MAN UP AND PADDLE!

A WILD AND DANGEROUS CIRCUMNAVIGATION AROUND IRELAND

by
Cathal McCosker

CU00858913

COPYRIGHT

REVIEWS

"A bold journey that stretched this duo to the physical limits –
but they gained so much more in return..."

– Bear Grylls

"This is a must-read book. It's funny, it's true and it will make
you laugh!"

– Martin Clunes

"Dangerous – a must read."

– Rory Bremner

"A pipedream that became reality after 67 days of blood, sweat
and a few scrapes, around the hospitable Emerald Isle – earned a
place in the Guinness Book of Records."

– HELLO! Magazine

"It was the beauty of the Irish coast that grabbed them, its
wildlife, and the thought of soda bread, so good after a salty day
on the summer seas."

– The Daily Telegraph

"An excellent introduction to Ireland and captures the spirit of the
country well. One gets a good sense of the constantly changing
weather sweeping over varied landscapes and of an unspoilt land
rich in nature. What comes across strongly however, is the
warmth of the people and their ready acceptance of two
disreputable looking canoeists."

– Edward Barrington, Irish Ambassador to London

DEDICATION

This book is dedicated to Charlie, Henry and Kitty.
Make life an adventure and never, ever give up!

CONTENTS

FOREWORD

Thankfully I first met Cathal McCosker after he had undertaken this expedition, far too late for him to ask me to join him. Though I have a seafarer's pedigree – my grandfather was an admiral and an uncle, on behalf of the British Navy, beat up Icelandic fishing boats during the Cod War - I was violently seasick just looking at the cover photo for this book. I will just stick to horses.

This is the sort of thing people do as a mid-life crisis, and in that respect Cathal was old before his time. He was still a mere stripling when he undertook this journey but he managed to think up this unique challenge, way out of his comfort zone, to test mind and body and what an adventure it proved to be.

The expedition took two and a half months, was unscripted and unsupported, and they did not even carry a mobile phone which is just as well knowing how well most of them react when introduced to water.

It was a puritanical and brave approach around the coast on which even the mighty Spanish Armada floundered. Its unpredictability makes it a fascinating story; no two days were ever the same, with the ever-changing seas and weather and the next stop westwards, America. That, in my book, is tightrope walking over the Niagara Falls without a safety net.

To be in small kayaks in 40-foot sea swells off the West Coast of Ireland is on its own an extraordinary adventure. When they set foot on land, the vast majority of the coastal inhabitants of Ireland looked after these two adventurers as they would their own family. The warmth, generosity and humour of the Irish, of which he is one, comes across over and over again in stark contrast to the welcome they received when they were chased by mad cows in Connemara.

This is an inspirational book about two guys who just got up and went for it. Leon and Cathal travelled in sea kayaks carrying all their equipment. These one-man boats are designed to travel at sea, they have waterproof hatches to store food, clothes, and equipment. Their shape with turned up ends allows swift travel through water, averaging 3/4 miles an hour. They cooked mainly porridge on a small stove, camping most nights around the coast. It is pure escapism, a journey around one of the roughest and most beautiful coastlines in the world. On the way they became feral, were robbed, suffered illness, were stung by jellyfish, jammed with Donovan & The Clancys, were washed out to sea and stayed with many, many generous hosts including the last Knight of Glin in a Castle. One of the joys of this trip is that these two guys carry very little in the way of possessions but are rich in spirit. This is a must-read book. It is funny, it happened, it makes you laugh out loud and cheers the spirit. They even made it into the Guinness Book of Records and Cathal was invited to give a lecture to the Royal Geographical Society in London. Those two facts alone qualify their wonderful trip as a serious undertaking.

By Marcus Armytage - Racing Correspondent, *Daily Telegraph*

INTRODUCTION

HELICOPTERS AND R.N.L.I.

"I'm so cold," Jim said, his head bent over my canoe, teeth chattering. Then he spewed, white and brown liquid forced from his mouth again and again. "Jim, are you okay to paddle?" I said. He was shivering more now, his eyes looked dull and distant. I reached for his boat to steady him.

"What's happening Cal, why aren't we getting anywhere? We've been paddling towards land for ages, it's still miles away," he spoke, looking for reassurance. I could give him none, for I knew as little.

One of the instructors was way in front, with some of our party. Delaney, the other, was about 500 to 600 metres behind and wouldn't speak. I was feeling bloody cold, I'd stopped shivering now. I knew this meant I was becoming even colder, one's body shivers in a final attempt to warm up, then after a while it gives up and stops. I'd capsized earlier, into the freezing cold water (off the Stacks, on the Anglesey coastline). At first I couldn't breathe, just coughed and spluttered with icy shock. I was wearing two t-shirts, a plastic windproof and shorts. Foster and Delaney had said: "You'll be fine, we're only going out for a short sea trip." That was nearly nine hours ago. We were now, all eighteen of us, out at sea losing sight of each other and the Anglesey coastline. There were only three in our group who'd been in a canoe before. What were we doing at sea? Why not a calm pond or something?

From the initial sunshine of a summer's day and safety of a calm bay, we were now in pouring rain and being washed out in an ever-increasingly rough sea. I would rise on a wave's crest and Jim disappeared in its trough. All I could think of was: am I going to die out here?

"Why don't they put a flare up; how bad does it have to get? I mean Jane's over there out of her boat. What the fuck is going on?" Jim shouted, frustrated and scared, only just able to paddle now his arms were beginning to seize up.

I didn't answer, I was praying. I don't know why. I'm not really a believer, but I was so shit scared that I was willing to try anything. I have to say it gave me some comfort and something to think about rather than the cold and fear I was feeling.

"Jim, Jim!" I shouted. "Look up... up!" I could see a yellow helicopter overhead.

"Is it for us? Do you think it's for us?" Jim shouted.

"I don't know, how did they know we were here?" I questioned. I didn't quite believe our situation was serious enough to warrant this kind of attention. This sort of thing happened to other people on the nine o'clock news, not us.

Before I knew it, Jim and I were on a winch, being drawn up into the helicopter. Jim was still vomiting, but nothing was coming out. The noise of this thing was incredible muting any conversation. Hand signal communication with the pilots was all we could manage, but we were safe, all 18 of us. Some were on the threshold of losing consciousness and their life. Most, however, bounced back after a warm hospital bed and plenty of hot tea and toast. A few were kept in for a couple of days. Everyone was worried about Jane; she just sat staring into space. "She's in shock," they said. "She'll be okay."

It was two years later when Leon and I met, while I was working on a summer vacation, as an Outdoor Instructor. I was a twenty-year-old student, at the time training to become a teacher (Physical Education and Biology), very carefree and at the age when you never listen to advice! Ending up, more often than not, wishing you had. Leon was a rather reserved trainee instructor, who had just discovered the magical effects of beer and women. A cocktail he was still perfecting! By the end of that summer season we were impossible dreamers. Always putting bizarre challenges and ideas together.

This trip all began, as most things of this nature invariably do, in a pub over a pint or two. Both of us were keen to go on an expedition that was a challenging adventure. We had often talked of paddling around Ireland, but had not felt ready for the rough and bleak seas we were likely to encounter on such a voyage. Fortified with Murphy's by the time we left the pub we'd decided to attempt it, both agreeing the underlying foundation to this adventure lay in having an open-minded approach all the way round. Getting involved, meeting locals, seeing Ireland's history, culture and music. The trip was to involve all this and the vehicle we would travel in, would be the sea canoe. I'm not sure if, at this stage, we were both egging each other on, waiting for the more sensible one to say "Okay, a joke's a joke."

It was not until nearly five years later - at this stage Leon was a senior instructor and I was teaching at Eton College - that we sat down and I really planned what I'd have to do. I say 'I', because one of Leon's qualities is that he's a lazy bastard and it would be me who put the trip together.

The list seemed endless. After a year of planning, re-planning, thinking and re-planning it all again, eventually we were ready to go. Our intended route was to start at Rosslare Harbour go clockwise, taking in the revered West Coast seas early in the trip when we would be relatively fit. The boats had been ceremoniously painted in green, white and gold – the flag of Ireland. We were almost self-sufficient, apart from food that we'd pick up en route. Everything we'd need was packed onto our boats.

Finally I decided to spend my saving on a waterproof video camera to enable us to catch highlights of our once-in-a-lifetime adventure and arranged to meet up with some Etonians en route. They were coming over to film parts, for a planned documentary-type film. That was it: we were off!!!

CHAPTER 1

VIRGIN PADDLERS

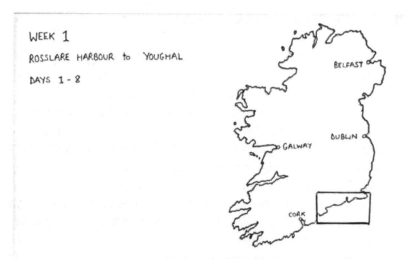

WEEK 1
ROSSLARE HARBOUR to YOUGHAL
DAYS 1 - 8

BELFAST

DUBLIN

GALWAY

CORK

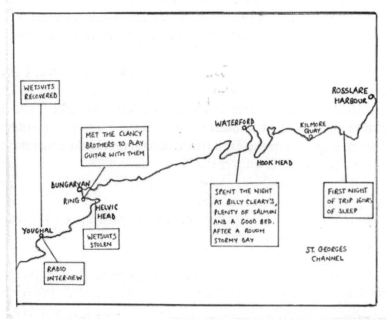

WETSUITS RECOVERED

MET THE CLANCY BROTHERS TO PLAY GUITAR WITH THEM

WATERFORD

ROSSLARE HARBOUR

KILMORE QUAY

HOOK HEAD

DUNGARVAN
RING

HELVIC HEAD

SPENT THE NIGHT AT BILLY CLEARY'S, PLENTY OF SALMON AND A GOOD BED. AFTER A ROUGH STORMY DAY

FIRST NIGHT OF TRIP 18HRS OF SLEEP

YOUGHAL

WETSUITS STOLEN

RADIO INTERVIEW

ST. GEORGES CHANNEL

Saturday 2nd July

Rosslare to the Beach near Lady's Island Lake. Distance: 10 miles. Duration: 4 hours. Sea state: choppy. Weather: F2, fog covering.

Our heads still spinning, we unloaded laden boats to applause and wolf whistles from Ireland's all-female rugger team, as they sped off the ferry in their orange and green minibus. This initiated much more horn honking and the like from other ferry passengers. Putting our craft to one side, we went in search of breakfast. It lay only 160 yards away, but in our path were large juggernauts, buses and a train track. We mastered all this, had breakfast and were back at our boats ready to go just as the ferry we'd arrived on set off back to Fishguard.

We pondered, looking for a spot to launch our boats off this rather large jetty. Our pondering was interrupted by a ginger-haired, red-faced ferryman.
"Are you fellas canoeing then?" he enquired.
"Yes," I said proudly, "we're going to circumnavigate Ireland."
"You are not, are ya?" he said, not knowing if we were serious or joking.
"I promise you we are," I said. "The only thing is we can't get started as there's nowhere to launch."
"Oh, that's no problem, sure I'll lower the loading ramp." And off he went towards some buttons. Before we knew it, the water was at our feet. On putting the boats in, we were both concerned at how deep they were both sitting in the water. What with guitars, golf clubs, and the rest of our miscellaneous cargo, the canoes were in fact only just floating.
"Be Jesus, ye look as if you've sunk before ye've been," said our ferryman, looking concerned.

A week or so ago, we'd been in the Peterborough column of the Daily Telegraph as they'd found our expedition a bit of a conundrum. I kept the sarcastic cutting. Looking at our boats and the ambitious task that lay ahead, their sarcasm seemed justified!

Leaving the cover of Rosslare's harbour walls, both in high

spirits even if a little tired, I wondered what lay ahead on this expedition and more importantly would I cope with it.

As expected, this first stretch of coast was quite uninspiring. It was a continuous line of flat sand beach in front and behind, no cliffs, fields nor landmarks to focus on or dream about. At times it was as if our boats weren't moving, just sitting. The sun sparkled momentarily, giving way to a hazy mist and drizzle. The noise of the dumping surf and seagulls screaming let you drift and relax into a daydream world of your own.

At the end of our first day, landing caused a few problems. The four-foot dumping surf, swirling within a mass of sand and seaweed, engulfed our boats. It turned them side on, throwing them onto the beach, luckily missing some rocks. Both of us completely soaked, violently shaking in a piercing cold wind, very quickly pulled on warm clothes.

It was our first night. Leaving the boats pulled high on the beach, I climbed the high sand dunes, making my way through harsh thistle to find a campsite. I'd managed to muffle my ears from the noise of the wind and dumping sea, by pulling my hat down around them, then making a second soundproof layer with my jacket hood. I was feeling quite jumpy ~ yesterday at school I was in a warm, safe environment. Now today, I was beginning the journey of a lifetime into the unknown, cold and wet. Making my way down to where a flat grassy area lay, I disturbed a rabbit. It darted out and again disappeared into the undergrowth, giving me a fright exaggerated by my anxiety and fatigue. I stood shaking for a moment, regaining composure and continued: "this will do nicely." It was sheltered, well-drained and flat - even the scout leader, Baden-Powell, would have approved.

Leon and I sat, eating a concoction of pasta, enriched by the wind's ingredients of sand and seaweed. It was a bleak and unsatisfying spot. It didn't matter, as both over-tired, we lay down and drifted into slumber. I awoke in darkness, still fully clothed and in the same spot outside the tent. I was concerned about our boats being washed away, a paranoia I hoped would disappear as the trip progressed. I went to look. The wind and sea's sounds were exaggerated in darkness: our boats were just as they'd been left.

Sunday 3rd July
Beach near Lady's Island Lake to Fethard. Distance: 15 miles. Weather: south-westerly F3.

We awoke, only just, I might add, at around 9.00 a.m. We'd slept from 5.00 p.m. the day before, giving us 16 hours sleep. I think this is a measure of how tired we were after the last few days. Rushing around chasing our tails and the ferry-crossing escapade.

After looking outside the tent, the view hadn't changed: it was still dull and rather depressing. We'd decided today was the day to get stuck into the mileage and find a more scenic Irish coast. We had a quick breakfast of two jam butties and sand, and headed away from this eerie place. The waves were still dumping as we launched.

The fog thickened, only allowing 400 yards or so of vision. Our spirits were still high, even though hungry for a sight of something. Our bodies were also hungry for fuel. Eventually, after almost giving up hope of ever seeing land or people again, a quaint beach and harbour came into view.
"You're in Kilmore Quay, lads," came the thick Irish voice as we pulled our boats up, "and if I were you, I'd stay, looking at that sea fog. Have ye come far in those yocks?"
"Rosslare," said Leon, "we're hoping to go a little further though."
"By Jesus, that's a fair old journey, I'd say. Anyway I'm Ivor," he said, reaching out his warm dry hand. "Ivor Sutton. Can I give ye's a cup-a-tae, warm ye up?" He pointed out his house overlooking the quay, and we followed him up.

We stood dripping on his kitchen floor, while Ivor unconcerned, ushered us to seats whilst casually laying the table. His interest was purely on making sure we were well-fed and engrossed in conversation.

"Ah Efa, come over and meet these two canoeists, sure they're going around Ireland." His daughter entered the kitchen.

"Well Jesus, rather you pair than I," she said, taking a place at the table.

Our eyes were almost popping out of our heads as we feasted on fresh crab and soft soda bread. The kitchen was quite modern in comparison with the rest of the house. The walls were all crooked with age, adding character. Every other room was in the middle stage of redecoration and restoration. It had possibly been in this state for some time; nothing seems to happen quickly in Ireland.

Upstairs in the sitting room, the walls were covered in Ivor's own paintings. He explained, "Ah sure, it keeps me busy on the wet days and by God we have enough of dem."

We left Ivor and Efa standing on the beach. We were now heading for Fethard, about 10 miles away. The first eight would be sand boredom, and the last two, pretty scenery they'd told us. Still misty and drizzly, we were back en route.

The harbour at Fethard encompassed a strong smell of rotting fish and crab. The water was crystal clear, the sandy seabed was littered with crabs' legs, toes and shells - I presume discarded by fishermen, once the meat was gathered. On the surface was a thick, multi-coloured film of oil. It led, like a path, to a fishing trawler's engine spout.

An old couple sat in their car looking out to sea, occasionally watching our movements. I caught the driver's eye; half-dressed, I made use of this passing glance. I walked over to the car and started a conversation. I was quite tired and ravenous: our conversation moved on from the kayaks and weather to food. As I had hoped, they offered us a lift to the pub some four miles away.

The pub was in darkness, only two candles on the bar for light. A power cut had struck. Worse still, no power, no food. We tracked back to the harbour. The hunger pangs had gone now.

18

It's funny how after a while that happened: all I wanted was to lie down and sleep. We threw our bags down in the darkness of the pot store, a decrepit small building which was ripe with the insipid smell of rotting fish. I forced my nose into my hat and soon fell into a deep slumber.

Monday 4th July
Fethard ["By Hook or by Crook"]. Distance: 12 miles. Sea state: flattish. Weather: F2 – 4, southerly.

I was drawn from sleep by a feeling of acute hunger; a feeling wasted as we had no food on board. Once my eyes, puffed and piggy, opened I was shocked into sitting up by the sight of rotting fish heads and crab toes all around me. The insipid stench was detected all too quickly by my uncovered nose. It acted like smelling salts to a dosing fainter. We were both up and out, packed and at sea, in lightning time. My hunger, took second place to the stench, now left behind, which would not go away. It worsened as time passed.

The day was sunny, the coastal scenery jagged and our mood was gay (if I'm allowed to say that, without casting doubt on my sexuality). After rounding Crook Head, before pulling to Dunmore East Yacht Club, I was intrigued by a bushy-bearded Robinson Crusoe "look alike" relaxing on the deck of a small 17 - 18 foot yacht. On taking a closer look, this boat really conjured up ideas of sailing off around the world – self-contained freedom. It turned out our Crusoe was a cabinet-maker from Wales, whom, sick of splinters in his fingers, was sailing around Ireland with his live-in lover Cheryl, a typist from Basingstoke. I know our canoes are self-centred freedom, however the yacht just added a touch of comfort.

Our boats only barely out of the water, we jumped onto the slipway, and within minutes had porridge bubbling on the stove. We were both so ravenous we did nothing but watch the food cook, then devoured it like two wild men. No conversation, just grunts and swallows. This seemed to amuse a gathering crowd of sailors. The onlookers edged slowly closer.

"Be Jesus, I wouldn't have come any closer, while you were feeding. For fear you might turn and eat myself, eh Patric?"

"You're damn right, 'twas like watching wolves." The two onlookers laughed loudly.

"Do you fellas need a warming or shower? Come on up and use the yacht club."

We declined the shower option, as wild we were and wild we would stay. Instead, we enjoyed some hot tea. I was told a piece of trivia, by the harbour master at Dunmore East, which I've since told almost everyone I know, so I might as well tell you.

Captain Cook, the swashbuckling pirate, many many moons ago had decided to set sail and invade, pillage and rape Ireland. The key to his plot was Waterford Bay: the front door, in those distant days, to this land. With a couple of failed attempts, he took out his map to re-plan the invasion. After much deliberation, his fist thumped the table. He stood and bellowed in triumph: "I'll take Waterford by Hook or by Crook." The two headlands he was referring to enveloped Waterford Bay - Crook Head and Hook Head. And so that's where the age-old expression originated from. To crown it all off, his invasion plan worked.

As we came out of the harbour, a south-westerly wind got up, blowing directly in our faces. The sea was choppy, its swell and waves were rather large and unfriendly. We battled on, and it was obvious to both of us that the storm was getting worse. It climaxed as we came around the headland. The waves were 8 to 12 feet high, swallowing us up as we paddled to survive. I saw a monster wave break right on Leon's boat, but amazingly he was still upright. We knew from our charts there was a small sheltered cove lying about half a mile away, so we headed for it. The wind was still building now, reaching the point, forward movement was almost impossible. We had to find that cove, soon. With the wash and spray it was difficult to make out any gaps in the coast's cliff face. Even though we were only 50 feet from it.

"I can see it," Leon shouted. It was about 400 yards away. Its mouth was tiny and not sheltered. Surf was rolling in, breaking

20

just where we would enter. It was our only option - so gritting our teeth, Leon and I went for it, just managing to control our surfing boats through the entry to the cove and sheltered water.

It was like entering a different world. The high cliffs removed the harsh wind and the sea's noise. All I could hear was paddle blade against water. On land, within a few minutes we had changed into warm clothes. I couldn't even hear a bird singing, just sweet calming silence. Our boats lay on a sand and rock beach, the kit hanging on a nearby fence and we sat side by side, propped up by a ditch eating a banana. In front I could see three houses, one quite new and still being built, the other falling down and the third a converted air-raid shelter type thing. The former and latter had sweet-smelling turf smoke rising from their chimneys. Needless to say, we were already forming a plan on how to introduce ourselves to the inhabitants and chance a warm cuppa and seat in front of the fire.

We need not have bothered. Before we'd even finished our bananas, Bill Cleary, a retired schoolmaster had introduced us to his wife, fire, and of course himself. He was proud to tell us we were not the first canoeists he'd rescued from the cold. Two years ago, on a very wet stormy night whilst out for a stroll, he had spotted and rescued by swimming and wading a girl and a man in a two-seater canoe. She had lost the power of her arms, and her companion was close to exhaustion, when Bill roped and pulled them in. Then he administered a bed and spuds to revive the half-drowned wretches. By comparison we were less of a shock, but he was no less of a host. He invited us to stay in the family caravan at the top of his field. What luxury: warmth, sea view and a chance to play the almost-forgotten guitars for the first time on the trip.

There was a rap on the caravan door. "Now lads, would ye come up the street and meet old Joe. He's an ole fella with no legs. He'll be pleased to see ye," Billy said opening the door.
"Sure, let's go," I said.

As we entered his humble home, we were welcomed by a yellow

glow of an open-hearth fire burning turf; the pleasant aroma filled the room. In the corner was a table with a two-ring stove and black kettle on top. The other end of the room had a small single bed in it. The walls were covered in postcards and pictures of local characters. The floor was littered with pots, old fishing nets, a water bucket and other odds and ends. There were no chairs, but stumps of wood to sit on. The whole one-room house was untouched by progress. We sat enchanted.

Tuesday 5th July
Rathmoylan (B.Cleary) to Annestown. Distance: 12 miles. Weather: F3 – 4, south-westerly. Sea state: choppy.

The day started with Leon strumming his beloved "Fender" guitar. As I vaguely flitted in and out of consciousness, I could feel the sun warming my face through the caravan window. I slowly sat up and reached out to my guitar to join this morning music. It would be one of the last times these guitars would be played on this musical journey. The fact is our naive romantic notion of carrying the guitars strapped to the back of our canoes was dangerously flawed. The wind kept catching our elevated hulls, making it difficult, at times impossible, to move in a straight line. Worse still, we, neither of us could roll nor rescue with the cumbersome weight. All in all, too dangerous. Billy had agreed to keep them for us until we, or someone, would collect them. Hopefully we would see them again en route!

The offer to stay another night was mulled over. We were both very tempted, but guilt got the better of us, as miles needed to be made. The weather was still quite shitty, but not enough to quit for a day. Especially as we'd just eaten a bucket of porridge and what seemed like a never-ending Irish fried breakfast. The plates were huge, the size of dustbin lids.

We set off into a south-westerly wind blowing directly into our faces. It was going to be another long haul to the next destination, wherever that might be. It was noticeable we were now relaxing into a routine of packing, canoeing and drifting into our own thoughts: a bit like the routine of going to work each day.

Enriched by the green fields and rocky shores, the day drifted to evening and then nightfall. I was beginning to really love the careless freedom I'd so craved and hoped I'd find on this trip.

Wednesday 6th July
Annestown to Dungarvan. Duration: 4 hours. Sea state: choppy. Weather: F3 – 4, south-westerly and rain.

It took four hours of grit and hard work to get to Helvic Head. It was the first real open crossing of the trip. Open, because we did not hug the shore or coast. Instead we cut across a bay two miles out at sea. This wasn't as daunting as you might think. True, it would take 40 minutes or so to reach land in an emergency. However, it was a calculated risk and with two of us, we felt mutual support from the other. The blind leading the blind, if you like!

Helvic was right on the headland. Its harbour was built like a Norman fortress. Even for a harbour its walls were extremely thick, made of large red blocks pinned by wood directly onto steel. Being situated directly on the headland, it must experience ferocious winter seas and storms. The entrance was so tiny and looked in on itself, again for protection, it was almost concealed. Once inside, the water was green with lines (or pools) of engine oil floating through it. The most noticeable difference was that the water was flat and still, like a village pond on a summer's afternoon. Unlike the rolling seas outside, the air - like most fishing ports - was full of a fishy smell, with the occasional whiff of diesel fumes. Not how you'd imagine the fresh sea air! Edging closer to one of the slipways, numerous boats with their painted hulls scarred with rust, were chugging and making ready to leave and fish. I could see numerous men washing, hosing, carrying and lifting. We glided by the slipway covered in green slippery algae and weed. I imagined all the colours and shapes in this harbour would be an artist's dream.

Even with the rain teeming down on us we were in good humour, although again ravenously hungry. This marked the premature start of our first day off (tomorrow), so the boats would sit for two nights unpaddled. Once changed, both crouching to avoid most of the lashing rain I had in one hand a hunk of cheddar, in the other half a loaf of bread. Each hand alternatively supplied my mouth. I had been eating and eating since the start of this expedition: it was like throwing a glass of brandy into a barrel of salt, trying to assuage my ferocious appetite.

The nearest town Dungarvan was about 10 miles away. So packing our deep jacket pockets with our wallets and worldly possessions, we set off bulging, on a winding uphill road away from the sea. Our legs hadn't had much exercise since we started. They had done some work whilst in the kayak, but very limited. Even after only six days, I noticed how weak they felt. As we walked, the rain subsided and the sun broke through. From the top of this hill, we had a clear view of the sea. It looked calm and inviting - a deceptive vision, as we knew it was rough and windy, and not a day to go for a dip.

We were now on the main road to Dungarvan trying to hitch a lift. The rain had started again, as car after car passed us by. Looking like two drowned rats, we took shelter under a bush outside a big pink bungalow. There would appear to be many pink bungalows in Ireland; it was almost a status symbol.
"Would you like to stand in the porch? It's warm and dry," came a lady's voice from behind us.
"Thanks," Leon began, "but we're hitching to Dungarvan."
"Oh, in that case jump in," she said, holding a van door open. "We're heading in that way, too." Without hesitation, we jumped in. As we drove along, we discovered Mrs McCavoy was the proud mum of 10 children. She went on to explain: "As they grew up, Patric, their father, and I have encouraged them all to play a different instrument." From the oldest who was 19 and played the banjo, right down to the two-year-old, who played the tin whistle. In effect, the parents had produced a traditional Irish band. This was an opportunity not to be missed, so I asked boldly if we could call in on our way back and hear them in action. "Sure, of course you can," she replied.

24

Dungarvan was a pretty town, although full of cars and people rushing about. The side streets, coffee shops and bars were more relaxed. The harbour itself housed The Moorings, a pub the sailors of tall ships in days of old would use. After many months at sea, their legs would uncontrollably sway and wobble. To help them stand still, around the pub counter was a brass bar which these sailors would cling to, whilst drinking ale.

It was about seven when we knocked on the McCavoys' door.
"You're welcome, go on through," said Mrs M., pointing the way to the sitting room. Within minutes the whole family had out banjos, tin whistles, Irish pipes, Irish drum, guitars and accordions: we were jamming and singing for around two hours. These instruments filled the room with a hail of poetic and traditional music played by children hardly out of nappies. The mandolin player was only seven years of age, but the sounds he produced were much older. I hate the idea of a video camera - I feel a bit of a tourist - but on this occasion I was very pleased to be able to capture the moment, something I hoped to do again and again on this voyage.

Thursday 7th July
Helvic Head to Ring, Dungarvan. Rest day. Sea state: calm. Weather: F1, southerly.

It was our first day off on the trip. The weather was foul - rain and hail and more rain. This, though, turned out to our advantage. Whilst taking in the air, strolling toward Dungarvan, who should stop to offer us a ride in his car but Bobby Clancy, of the legendary Irish folk group, The Clancy Brothers.
"Ah, sure this day's only fit for drinking and music. Would ye's join me in a drop. Put the life back in ya, be God," he said, flicking the windscreen wipers onto fast.
"I'm in."
"And me," I replied.
In we walked, and a cloud of tobacco and turf smoke engulfed us.
"Hey ho, how's Bobby?" came a cry from the corner.
"Yes, Pat, have the fiddle with ye. These fellas are on a musical journey around our green isle," Bobby bounced back.

"Be Jesus, are dey now. I have it wit me," came the reply.

"Margaret - the back room!" Bobby shouted across the bar at the landlady. The four of us followed Bobby along passages and through doors until we came to another smaller bar with hard seats, fire burning and two wrinkly men sitting in the corner, peering over their pints.

"Margaret we'll have four hot whiskeys - and would you phone home. Tell them to send Efa and Pat down with any of the others that want," Bobby said, leaning on the bar whilst reaching over for a banjo.

"Right ye are," came her reply.

"Now lads," Bobby started turning towards us, banjo in hand. "We'll have a bit of a crack."

A few moments later, the landlady placed the hot toddies on the table saying:

"Efa and Pat are on their way; Maggie's coming, as well Bob."

"God love ye, you're the bringer of good news, so ye are," Bobby replied, lifting his glass for a toast. "Slaine and safe journey."

"Slaine," we three replied, meaning 'good health' in Gaelic.

It was soon after that music and song began, and I again resorted to being a tourist with the video camera. Within a short time the back room was packed with more musicians, locals and anyone else who was around. Rain continued to pour as we bathed in hot whisky and culture.

CHAPTER 2

WILD MEN APPEAR

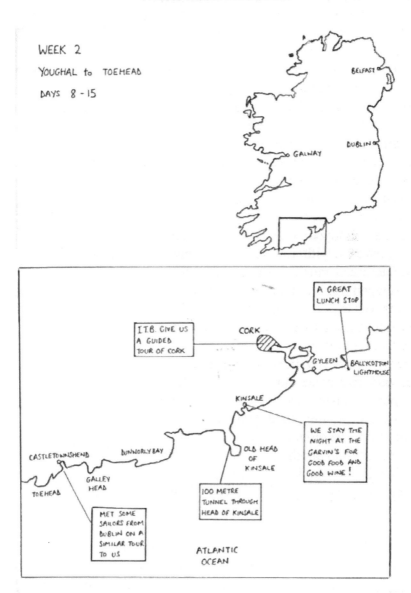

WEEK 2

YOUGHAL to TOEHEAD

DAYS 8 - 15

BELFAST

DUBLIN

GALWAY

A GREAT
LUNCH STOP

I.T.B. GIVE US
A GUIDED
TOUR OF CORK

CORK

G'YLEEN

BALLYCOTTON
LIGHTHOUSE

KINSALE

WE STAY THE
NIGHT AT THE
GARVIN'S FOR
GOOD FOOD AND
GOOD WINE !

CASTLETOWNSHEND

DUNWORLY BAY

OLD HEAD
OF
KINSALE

GALLEY
HEAD

TOEHEAD

100 METRE
TUNNEL THROUGH
HEAD OF KINSALE

MET SOME
SAILORS FROM
DUBLIN ON A
SIMILAR TOUR
TO US

ATLANTIC
OCEAN

Friday 8th July

Helvic Head to Youghal Bay. Distance: 20 miles. Duration: 5 - 6 hours. Sea state: calm. Weather: southerly F3 - 4.

After much itching and almost uncontrollable scratching throughout the night, I'd come to the conclusion - or even realisation - that in seven days and seven nights I had neither bathed, showered nor shaved. I looked in the mirror today for the first time and decided Leon and I had become or reverted back to wild men. Our eating habits reflected it and our craving for bananas proved it. We were even calling each other "wild man" and responding to each other in grunts and ritual bellows. If this was happening after one week at sea, I feared the events to follow.

We had enjoyed such fun and frolics in Helvic, Ring and Dungarvan - with the marvellous hospitality measured in tea, Guinness and music - it was sad to leave and even sadder when we noticed our wetsuits were missing. They were very important bits of kit: they acted as a neoprene shield guarding us from cold seawater. Luckily, the rest of our gear lay untouched.

There were a few fishermen mending nets at the bottom of the harbour. We made our way down. "Hi fellas, you haven't seen a couple of wetsuits about? Only ours seem to have gone missing," I said. Not wishing to accuse anyone.
"No, not I," said one.
"Nor me," said another.
"What did they look like?" asked the third.
I explained where we'd left them and how all the other gear was intact.
"They'll be gone - some wee bastard - you can't leave nothing down," the first one began. "Well fuck, aren't these rare times on the Head, for some wee hare to be taking what isn't theirs!" The fishermen were furious that one of their colleagues had stolen as they put it "the safety of another seafarer, putting life in danger." These men were so concerned they wanted to buy us new wetsuits. We politely declined. They were also embarrassed, almost ashamed, that we'd been robbed on their headland. We

almost felt guilty for telling them. Before we moved on, John Whelan (the first man we had spoken to) said: "Don't worry lad, I'll find the bastards and return the gear." We thanked him for his kind sentiment, but knew the kit was lost.

The water was reasonably calm and we made good headway. After about an hour, the wild man in us needed more fuel. We did not land - instead bobbing up and down holding each other's boat in a makeshift raft. After a couple of grunts and swallows we'd devoured two fruit cakes, two Twixes and a packet of Custard Creams. We were still surprised by the amount we were eating. It was easily double our normal intake. It was three and a half hours plodding along before we came to Ardmore: here, we stopped for lunch and rest in The Cup and Kettle. On entering this café there were loud, shrill giggles from behind the counter - girls laughing, quite plainly at us. I turned to Leon and he to me. We then also burst into laughter. We both looked so odd in our dripping wet canoeing gear, our matted hair, unshaven faces and salt-stained skin.

Before heading back to the beach, we had a stroll around. It was like a chocolate box village. The streets and walkways were clean and manicured. Flowers were hanging in baskets and every cottage was thatched and freshly painted. This extended lunch stop almost cost us dearly. For the second time that day we were being robbed, though not by man. This time, the sea was the culprit. The tide had come in and snatched our boats. They were about 100 yards offshore. A crowd of holidaymakers sat watching, as if waiting for the matinee performance to begin. Begin it did. "Shit, look at the tide - our boats!" Leon shouted, running towards the sea. I followed, splashing into the water at the same time. In all the excitement, I'd forgotten the groceries in my hand; very soggy groceries now. We made it to our boats, followed by rapturous applause and cheering from our audience. Our kit intact, pride dented, we paddled away - not feeling like an encore.

I spotted a beautiful small cove inside Youghal Bay. The sun was just setting as we landed on Cabin Point, taking particular care, as surf was bullying our boats towards sharp rock and reef. It was deserted apart from a handful of houses and thatched cottages above. Pulling on warm clobber we set about exploring, hoping to chance a cup of tea. We chatted to one of the very friendly locals, Willie, who invited us for a cuppa as soon as he'd mended his drainpipe. As this might take some time, we decided to chance our luck elsewhere and also find a campsite. We knocked on the door of Mr and Mrs Gibson, both holidaying in Ireland - they welcomed us in, dried us off, gave us ham sandwiches and Guinness. They also offered their meadow as a campsite.

Some people have an aura of calmness all around them and in their voice. Willie lived in a cottage on Cabin Point with his dog Be-Be, a Jack Russell full of life and boundless energy. His garden was full of oddments recovered from shipwrecks or else washed up on the beach. It was a fascinating and enchanting garden with everything from ships' lamps to plane wings decorating it. The inside was even more of a treasure trove: with numerous paintings and photographs; not to mention book after book all relating to the sea, its R.N.L.I. rescues and the shipwrecks along the south-west coast.

The glow of a warm, peat fire coloured the room. It had a particular smell, a bit like a pleasant joss stick or aromatherapy candle. Be-Be was sitting in front of it, chewing and wrestling with Willie's old boots. A birdcage was hanging from the roof with a fluffy plastic canary in it. I enquired. "Ah sure, it's less money than the real ting and ders plenty of birds singing in de garden," came Willie's reply.

The roof also housed a brass lantern, fishing float and numerous shells. The rest of the room was dominated by a breathtaking sea view, an ever changing portrait of nature and her inhabitants. Leon and I sat around the fire, while Willie sat opposite the window telling stories of the wrecks and men rescued around the Cabin Point.

Saturday 9th July

Cabin Point to Youghal. Distance: 3 miles. Duration: 2 - 3 hours. Sea state: rough. Weather: F7 - 8 gale, gusting; dropping to F5. Raining and dull sky.

I awoke in the Gibsons' meadow; it was around 7.30 am. I looked out of the tent - there was a hoolie blowing, easily gale force; the sea was covered by white horses riding the swell. I turned to Leon, but he was still sleeping. I rolled over and decided to do the same. When neither of us could sleep any more at around 10.00 a.m., we shook off our sleeping bags, brushed our teeth and headed up the meadow to the Gibsons, who'd offered us breakfast the night before. They were happy to see us - the way we looked, and probably smelled, I was amazed anyone would be happy to see us.

In typical wild man style we declined the offer of a shower, and launched straight into breakfast. Joan seemed rather concerned that the eggs might be over or under-done. She needn't have worried as they didn't even touch the sides.

It seemed this southerly wind was just blowing hard enough to confuse us as to whether to stay or push on, (after all, Donovan and a guide from the Irish Tourist Board in Cork were waiting to show us around.) We walked up to the headland to see how big the swell was before deciding. It was too big to paddle. So, frustrated we waited, hoping the storm would abate.

At 2.30 p.m., both eager to continue, we launched into rough seas. With hindsight, one could say it was a foolish move, as the sea canoeist is not equipped for such seas. At the time however, our will to move forward blinkered our common sense. Even the Gibsons and Willie were concerned and suggested waiting till the next day. We decided their naivety of the canoe, gave their opinions little weight. An arrogant view - anyone can see rough weather, canoeist or otherwise.

After my first paddle stroke I knew I'd made a mistake, but again arrogance persisted. Keeping very close (about two feet apart)

31

we battled for two hours, all the elements against us: wind, hail, tide and sea. Usually after two hours paddling with such ferocity, we'd have covered seven to eight miles. Today, however, only two. We were both soaked to the skin, getting cold, and only by our fingernails surviving. We could not go any further, pulling in at a break wall in Youghal Bay.

The very moment I pulled off my spray deck, I felt the cold air on my legs. Inside the boat the air was warmed by body heat and so rarely would we paddle with covering on our legs. Thus once out of the boat, they were immediately exposed, more often than not to cold wet rain.

Shivering, but happy to be back on land, we made for a very large, grey house.

By now we'd become so confident and used to the Irish hospitality, that we joked as we walked in: "Will it be salmon or fresh lobster for lunch?" Our dreamy thoughts were very quickly brought down to earth when the Swedish family in residence slammed the large oak door in our wet faces and sent us on our way.

Undeterred, we walked on in the pouring rain and howling gale. We'd warmed up a little, but were hungry. Neither of us knew what would happen next on this trip. It was a bit like being one of the Famous Five, with lashings of ginger beer, and adventure followed by adventure. "Yes, oh yes!" Leon shouted, pointing ahead. It was a group of canoeists. We both knew this meant there had to be an outdoor centre nearby and they would definitely take us in.

Within an hour, we were showered and seated cupping piping hot mugs of tea in our mitts telling everyone of our trip so far. We were given a key to Youghal Outdoor Centre by Ruth, the chief instructor, and told to make ourselves at home. We couldn't believe our luck again. What a superb place to wait out the storm. To crown things off, Youghal was celebrating the anniversary of the discovery of Sir Walter Raleigh's potato by having an Irish festival in the town.

The telephone was ringing. As we were the only ones in the place, Leon quickly flipped a coin to see who would go down the two flights of stairs to answer it. I lost. I picked it up to be told it was the coastguard. He'd had a call from a concerned lady, Joan, about two canoeists last sighted yesterday paddling in rough seas. He was about to alert a rescue and search. I explained who we were and that we were okay. I also explained we had distress flares and satellite distress signals with us. He was satisfied and said he would call Joan to put her mind at ease. It was good to know someone had their eye on us; we could so easily have needed rescuing yesterday.

Walking down the street, a car started honking its horn. The driver was waving at me. At first I wasn't sure what was going on. Then who should get out of the car but Tom Wheelan, the fisherman from Helvic Head, who had been really pissed when he'd heard about our wetsuits being stolen. Not only had he tracked us down, but he'd also tracked our wetsuits down,. "Now lads, the fellas dat had em won't do anytin the like that again, I can tell ya," he said. Truly amazing - it could only happen in Ireland!

Sunday 10th July
Youghal to Bally Gyleen (Dutch). Distance: 20 miles. Duration: 5 - 6 hours. Sea state: choppy. Weather: F5 dropping to F2.

I awoke with my first hangover. It all stems back to my upbringing as a polite well-mannered fellow, who when offered a drink does not wish to offend and feels obliged to accept. So, as many pints of Murphy's were offered, I accepted. Hence this painful head and foul-tasting mouth. And we all know that the only cure for such ailments is a huge fried breakfast of sausages, bacon, eggs and the like, all covered in ketchup and washed down with a pot of tea. With this in mind, we both hit a local cafe and took the cure.

At 10.30 a.m., Radio Cork phoned the centre and I did a live on-air interview with Alf. We discussed the paddling, our adventures and the Irish nation - quite a lot considering my delicate state.

After looking at the weather and sea regularly, at 1.00 p.m., it seemed to be clearing and the southerly wind was dropping. With this break in the weather we wasted no time, said our goodbyes, and were on the water by 1.30 p.m. paddling away from Youghal as if we owed money to someone on the quayside. We made good headway, stopping for food after three hours on an island at Ballycotton with a big red lighthouse at its centre. The actual lighthouse was set at the highest point on the island, standing proud and central. Around it were several cottages and outhouses, the remains of what used to be a small community living on and caring for the lighthouse, before they were automated. Many say this was the saddest day, when it came - for the lighthouse men were a constant look-out for sailors and canoeists at sea, now lost forever. Inside, the cottages still looked in use: coats hung up, boats in the corner and tables laid. The giveaway though was the musty scent hanging in the air. Outside, wild sheep and goats roamed, probably left over from this now dead community. I wanted to pitch our tent, but felt we needed to press on. It was a beautiful place though: I intend to go back one day.

Our meal had consisted of stale bread, at least six days old and an equally stale half-pot of pasta sauce. Both of us had again reverted back to wild men, so we ate ravenously. I was to regret this frivolous approach an hour later when this decaying sauce decided to reappear all over my spray deck, buoyancy aid and boat. It was like a pressurised tube of toothpaste exploding, but on a much larger scale. I did feel a lot better for it though. Wild man Leon felt no after-effects - his stomach is made of lead.

We landed at 8.15 p.m., very badly, on a dumping surf beach. If you are not a canoeist it's difficult to grasp how fraught with hazards and danger this is, not so much to yourself but your fibreglass boat and equipment - in this case, the video camera and its leaking case. Both of us landed quite badly and were lucky not to have damaged our boats. I was turned sideways and brought up the beach with Leon not far behind, eventually to crash into me. Obviously the Irish Sea isn't big enough for Leon. I'd hate to see him park a Ford Estate in London! In front of us lay a quaint, white and blue fisherman's cottage with smoke coming from its chimney. So being the chancers we've become, Leon knocked on the door to be received by an old and friendly Dutch man and his wife, Patricia, who invited us in, making us most welcome offering hot tea and showers.

We were the first visitors they'd had who'd actually come from the sea, they told us, as we sat warming ourselves next to the kitchen Aga. The cottage was very different to how you might imagine it after looking at the outside. It was very definitely European in style: lighting was all by table and standard lamps, the seating was very upright, paintings were of Mediterranean sunsets and beaches. Everything was neatly in its place. Don't let me mislead you into thinking it was a forbidding place. It was, on the contrary, warm and comfortable. It was, however, like being in France, or indeed, Holland.

The garden where we pitched our tent was small and cosy with a path leading to a stream. The thick surround of hedges and foliage made it a very peaceful and sheltered spot, perhaps contributing to our good night's sleep.

Monday 11th July
Gyleen to Crosshaven, Cork. Distance: 6 - 7 miles. Duration: 3 hours. Weather: F2 southerly.

We waved another set of new friends goodbye. They'd offered to put us up in their holiday home any time, in exchange for teaching them how to fish from a kayak, so we might well return!

Crosshaven is the home of the oldest yacht club in England or Ireland, the Cork Royal Yacht Club. Throughout this week, it was hosting its annual yacht regatta. Paddling across and into the mouth of Crosshaven, a light breeze was blowing with a warm glow from the sun. We were kept entertained by the sheer magnitude of this regatta. There were hundreds, if not thousands, of sailing boats ranging from small toppers to virtual ships.

On landing outside the Yacht Club, I thought, whilst tying our boats up, how tiny and inadequate they looked next to their big brothers of the sea. A bit like parking a Skoda next to a B.M.W. The atmosphere was one of hustle and excitement. People and children were everywhere. The club's facilities had been extended for the event, with marquees stretching for about a mile. These housed bars, restaurants, gift shops and the usual regalia of such events.

We left the yacht club by bus, going to Cork central bus station. I'd arranged to meet up with two bodies. The first was from the school I was teaching at: Eton's crack film crew. The second was an Irish Tourist Board guide, who was going to show us Cork's sights. The film crew were going to follow us for eight days, filming us on water and land to make a short film as a school project.

As we arrived, I could see the film crew and guide waiting. Our guide was dressed in typical green I.T.B. uniform. The film crew had travelled through the night to get to us and understandably were a bit tired. In fact, the crew driver was asleep standing up.

The I.T.B. guide showed us to her Citroen and we piled in: cameras, film, batteries, bags and all. It was a tight squash, but just manageable if I put my leg in the ashtray and face against the back window. It was like a Cook's tour - taking in cathedrals, prisons, and of course Blarney Castle, where we both kissed the Blarney Stone.

Leon and I returned, tired, to Crosshaven, not in the mood for hustle and bustle. We walked out of the main maze of streets. After an hour of searching, our only option in this relatively built-up area was to pitch a tent in someone's garden. We knocked on a door, to be told: "As long as there's no noise from you young fellas, that'll be grand."

36

I fell into slumber as soon as my head touched, I'd say the pillow, but we didn't have any so instead it was the ground. Not for long though: at around midnight, our door was unzipped and two young ladies peered in. "Lads," one said, with slurred speech, continuing, "Would ye's like a drink."

"Come into the house for a whisky," the other said.

Leon said nothing, just rolled over and carried on sleeping. I politely declined and too rolled over. "Come on, would ya," they came again, this time shaking Leon's leg. Leon rolled over and slowly sat up.

"No, no, really. It's really nice of you, but I have neither the energy or willpower to do anything but sleep, sorry," Leon said addressing his swaying beauties, a word I use loosely on this occasion. He then smiled, lay back, rolled over and went back to sleep. Our beauties moved on.

Alas, more interruptions: I awoke from a dream about a storm at sea, nose down in a puddle and water dripping on my head. The tent had sprung a leak, mainly on me. I was getting to that stage when lack of sleep makes one irritable and whingey. I moved from under the drips and tried again, writhing occasionally in my damp cocoon, too tired to investigate or move again. I don't think Leon stirred once, as I encroached on his sleeping space. I'm glad I've already cleared that sexuality business up in the previous chapter.

Tuesday 12th July
Crosshaven to Kinsale Harbour. Distance: 25 miles. Sea state: calmish/choppy. Weather: F2 southerly, very sunny and hot.

The weather today was reasonably calm and we made good speed, although never certain of when it would rain or indeed shine. We left with the film crew in tow in a small motorboat, bobbing up and down taking shots of our every movement. Even wild men grunting and eating seemed to be relevant. They disappeared after two hours and we were again on our own. Pulling in for a late breakfast, my legs unfortunately hadn't realised I was about to stand and exit my kayak. I went arse over head, straight into a cold Atlantic sea - Leon almost fell in with laughing at my blundering misfortune. I hate being in the sea when it's covered in weed and algae, the touch and feel of it against my skin, and not knowing what's hiding in it, awakens my paranoia.

Today, the combination of colder weather and the intense amount of time we've spent reliant on each other helped fuel another argument. It all started when Leon launched first after breakfast. Usually we wait for each other, but Leon just paddled on. This meant I had to work hard to catch up. It was something right from the onset of this expedition, that we'd said we would not do.

I found out later he was sick and bored of my conversation, wanting a break. At the time I didn't see it that way. I was becoming tired of always clearing lunch away and sick of his continued silence. I caught up eventually.
"Cheers for waiting, not," I said, emphasising the last word. There was silence. His reply was a half smile. This really pissed me off. We continued for over an hour without a word. I then suggested a chocolate break and he agreed. We stopped and I pulled out a bar, the last of our supply. It was then that I noticed chocolate on his face. He'd already had a bar, offering me none and saying nothing: I saw red.
"You selfish, self-centred bastard - you've had a choccy stop!" I blasted.
"Oh fuck off, just fuck off," he responded, which made a change.
"You piss me off - me, me, me. Take, take, take. I'm so piss sick of your selfish attitude!" I shouted.
"My attitude! All you do is bore me fucking senseless, talking at me - shit, shit! You make me want to vomit. I paddled ahead to get a break from you," he said.
"Yeah, leaving me once again to clear up your fucking mess," I returned.
"Oh fuck off," he finished, paddling away.
Neither of us spoke again. We'd both clearly said our piece and got out our frustration. The air was again clear. We would tiptoe around each other for a few hours, being politically polite, and then fall back into our more familiar friendly and compromising repose.

The day ended three-and-a-half hours later when we pulled in, pretty exhausted, at a slipway leading to a quiet pub, The Bulman. After a pint, we called up the Garvin family, whose son I'd taught. I had been told they lived in the area and would hopefully offer to put us up for the night. We got more than we had bargained for. Michael Garvin picked us up and drove us back to their holiday home, Sandy Cove House, set in an idyllic natural harbour with a view untouched by man, full of nothing but fresh sea air. We were both treated to a steaming hot bath. I decided it was time to rid myself of my wild man hairs and have a shave; I could again see my face. I'd like to say a pretty sight, but frankly I think it was whacked with the "ugly brush" at birth. Our bedroom overlooked the dreamy harbour. The sash window was partly open, and through it came the aroma of food being barbecued below.

The evening was light and warmer than the day. The Garvins had invited numerous guests to their soiree. All were English living and working in Kinsale. Kinsale is almost the 'little England' of Ireland. Many Brits holiday there in their second homes or sailing boats. Kinsale is also known for its equestrian events and its beautiful harbour full of very keen sailors. I retired full and content to a warm and comfortable bed. A contrast, I thought, to the previous night.

Wednesday 13th July
Kinsale, Sandycove House to Seven Heads, Dunworly Bay. Distance: 23 miles. Duration: 6 - 7 hours. Sea state: calm. Weather: F1 sunny, hot and blue skies.

I awoke from my deep slumber to the smell of smoky bacon. I did wish I didn't have to paddle today. I dreamt of being able to roll over and go back to sleep. But alas, it was not to be. I arrived in the kitchen only moments later to devour bacon and eggs.

Once out on the water, I was content. It had taken a great deal of energy to get there: packing, changing, unpacking, checking charts, routes and so on. This was probably the best weather we'd had so far - warm and sunny. The sea was mild, hardly a ripple. It was perfect for what we wanted to try and do today. Again, the film crew followed alongside as we paddled.

We had been told the 'Oldhead of Kinsale' has a small hole going right through it - about 300 metres long. With a calm sea and low tide, it is possible to just get through it. First though, we had to find it. After entering a few caves with no luck, I came across a hole just wide and high enough for us to fit. Leon led the way, guided only by a light at, what we hoped was the end of the tunnel. It was completely dark. With our vision gone, the sounds of the sea became exaggerated, adding an air of tension. The walls were dark and slimy. I guessed the slime was the carpet of sea urchins covering it. It took two to three minutes before we emerged, almost blinded by the daylight sunshine and deafened by high-pitched birds toing and froing from their nests.
The high sea cliffs were completely covered by birds including: cormorants, shags, herring gulls, kittiwakes, oystercatchers, puffins and more. Every nook and cranny was engaged. The cliffs were white-washed with bird droppings; the smell was also very evident in the air. This explosion of nature took us both completely by surprise. Never before nor since have I experienced such a sight. We paddled around the birds for about half an hour watching them swoop and fish.

To watch a puffin fishing and then trying to take off with its catch is quite like a "Carry On" sketch. These are round, fat and clumsy birds. They carry their catch of small sprats clamped in their tiny yellow beaks. I noted that any more than three sprats in their beaks and take off was impossible. First, they paddled their short little feet and legs like stink, at the same time flapping their equally small wings. Then like a bouncing bomb, they bounced and bounced and bounced off the water until eventually they bounced high enough to stay up. If however they got greedy, they crashed, losing all their catch. I hope I've described it well enough for a picture to be conjured up. But really, to see it is to believe it.

Another bird, the fulmar has a unique method of keeping its nest safe. If any predators come too close it vomits over them: a sticky, smelly, strong fish-smelling, tar-like liquid. Not dissimilar to Leon after eight pints and a Vindaloo!

We crossed from Kinsale to our next point the Seven Heads - around 12 to 14 miles - without a portage (a canoeist's cool word meaning "to stop"). I was caught short. There was no option: I had to urinate in my boat. Something humiliating you might say, but we were wild men now. The initial feeling was quite warm and almost pleasant, though needless to say short-lived. I felt like a naughty child unable to make the loo in time. For the next two-and-a-half hours, cold smelly urine sloshed around my cockpit, thoroughly soaking my skin and wetsuit. Urine in your boat and sodden into your wetsuit isn't a serious problem. But urine can be a medium for numerous bacteria to grow, causing mild irritating rashes to painful infections. Usually, it would be possible to wash out the boat and wetsuit in fresh water and chlorine. Unfortunately neither was at hand on this trip. I would wash both in seawater, but expected a rash shortly. The urine would also attract numerous unsavoury insects into my boat. All rather tedious.

Passing the spot where the Lusitania went down, we paused. It was sunk by a German U-Boat in the Second World War - they believed it to be carrying U.S. troops and supplies. Evidence suggests many civilians were on board. Two seals were playing where it would have sailed all those years ago.

Landing this evening was very easy, making a pleasant change. Even whilst putting on warm kit it didn't rain, just a fresh breeze to dry our sodden clothing.

Both a little concerned because the film crew were not around, we pitched our tent high on an open hill to attract them. They were meant to meet up with us here in Dunworley Bay. As we sat waiting, and watching the tide roll in, four men (two skinny and bald, two pot-bellied and bald) jogged past us in the nude heading for a twilight dip. I persuaded Leon not to join them, as his street cred would take a pounding.

Thursday 14th July

Day Off. *Dunworley Bay. Distance: 0 miles. Sea state: calm and choppy. Weather: thick fog.*

I awoke this morning feeling tired, sunburnt and thoroughly drained. I poked my head out of the tent to spy a view strangled by fog: what a very depressing sight. After the usual dressing and teeth brushing, we both concluded that a day off was needed. The four miles to the nearest village, called Butlerstown, was a pleasant stroll. We didn't really speak. I was taking in the scenery from a new perspective, on land. Here, the only place open was a pub. It was a welcoming empty bar, full of character enriched with a smoky smell. I resisted the urge to order a pint of Murphy's and instead had a strong coffee. The landlady was taken by our dress: I guess fleeces, bright trousers and Jesus sandals are odd. But when both are identical, that's even odder. Our sponsors, understandably, gave us exactly the same kit. It's caused plenty of enquiries, comments and schoolgirl laughter. She came round the bar and sat down with us. "A ye travelling new agers?" she began. "I've not seen many dressed like that!"
"No, we're not. Anyway I think you mean 'new age travellers'," Leon politely corrected. "We're canoeing around Ireland," he said proudly.
"Which island? There are no islands around these parts."
"No, I mean the whole of Ireland," he explained.
"Well Jesus! Did ye hear dat Pat? Canoeing around our own Green Isle. They must be two tuff uns," she said.
"Well, they don't look it," said Pat, lifting his pint, one elbow leaning against the bar.
"Ah, away Pat, leave the lads alone. Take no notice." She waved her hand in defiance at Pat.
"He could be right - we haven't made it yet," I said softly.

We went on to explain that we were in a predicament, as we'd lost the film crew. "Right," she said, pulling car keys from her pocket. "Let's go and find them." So off we went. The car was full of empty Lucozade bottles. It had a cracked windscreen, and the masking tape holding it together impaired almost any vision. This didn't seem to bother our driver. The driver's seat refused to adjust, so changing gear for this rather slight lady was a major ordeal - as it was for the passengers, with the bumping and jerking that resulted. After about an hour of looking up, down and all around and thoroughly enjoying it, our chauffeur decided to come back and phone the Garda (the Irish police) to see if they might offer assistance. The sergeant, a pleasant fellow, assured me that if he saw them, he'd call us at the pub. But he explained: "I can't give it my immediate attention, as the cow has the skitter (diarrhoea) and I'm waiting on the Vit (vet)."

No sooner had I put the phone down than we were whisked into the landlady's private back room, seated in front of a warm, turf-burning fire and a plate of mashed potatoes, cabbage and bacon floating in onion gravy was thrust under our noses with the words: "Tuck in now boys." We could not have asked for any better food or treatment; she even put Neighbours on the telly to make us feel at home! Both of us had seconds, returning eventually to the bar for another coffee and read of the paper. Here we would stay until the crew arrived (or not, as the case might be).

I stirred from sleep to the sound of two children, something I was getting used to on this trip. At first I thought I was dreaming, but reality struck when a shake of the tent prompted many drops of condensation from the roof, bringing me abruptly into reality. It was a bit like having a glass of ice-cold water thrown into your face.
"Can I help you?" I croaked, sitting up.
"The film crew phoned - they're in Baltimore," the older girl confided, in a sweet Irish tone.
"Baltimore? Bloody Baltimore! Do they think we've got wings on our boats?" Baltimore was a good 50 miles away.
"They said they'd be leaving in the afternoon."
We thanked them for bringing the news, even as bizarre as it had been, and fell quickly back into our slumber.

Friday 15th July
Dunworley Bay to Toe Head Bay. Distance: 22 miles. Duration: 7 hours. Weather: F1 - sunny day.

I'd made it clear to the crew on both the Ordnance Survey map and chart that we would pull in and camp at Dunworley Bay. We spent a whole day waiting around for them, calling the Garda and so on. To find they were in Baltimore really pissed me off. This wasn't the first time we'd arranged to meet them and they'd not turned up. I was trying to put myself in their shoes, but still found myself cursing their irritating incompetence. The bottom line was they did not have any understanding of the expedition, and how it was mainly governed by the elements. After a chat with Leon, he agreed it was time to drop the film crew and instead film it ourselves with the waterproof camera, just as we'd previously been doing. It was hard enough paddling each day, without this added hassle.

Our bodies were now into the swing of paddling each day, .We still had the odd ache, but were most definitely becoming canoe fit. Both of us were finding lower back irritation. It manifested itself as pain when lying flat. We could only manage to sleep once we had been lying on our backs, knees bent, in the air for half an hour or so. Only then could we roll onto our sides and sleep. This must have been caused by our bent-forward position when paddling.

Leon was carrying a slightly worrying injury - a hernia. He assured me it should be okay, but the previous day he did confide it was giving him some discomfort. I hoped the day's rest would have helped. Leon had had this problem for over a year, while awaiting an operation, although he had still managed to play much sport.

The day was pleasant and sunny, full of high cliffs and beautiful scenery, wildlife and harbour bays, in one of which we had a short lunchbreak and sun snooze. The conversation - today mainly whingeing and moaning as you might expect - centred around the film crew and their seeming incompetence. Their presence was most definitely lowering our mood and taking something away from the freedom of sea kayaking, which was by definition to travel at will, with the real world left on shore in limbo. The sooner we got back to this the better. After seven hours paddling, we cruised into Toe Head Bay.

Toe Head Bay is a long, deserted, silent, sandy beach. There was only one house on our left, elevated by a hillside. After pulling our boats up, we chanced a closer look. Leon and I walked along an enchanted tunnelled path, leading to a set of steps, then into a green, walled garden, bordered by roses and lavender. The house itself was a large, white, two-storey typical Irish cottage, with red borders around the windows and front door. As we approached, we were spotted by two little girls playing in the garden.
"I'm eight years old, you know," one said, putting down her toys and approaching us.
"So am I," said the other.
"But she's oldest by a month." They led us to their mother. She was from Dublin, this being the "holiday" home. After a short chat, she pointed out a field to pitch our tent. The two girls escorted us, fascinated by our kit and boats. Once the tent was pitched both girls, now joined by their young cousin, played in their new "Wendy House"!!! Meanwhile, we relaxed on the beach, cooking porridge in the evening sun.

After the usual visit to the local pub, we returned to our tent under the cover of darkness. Both shattered, we were in our bags and ready to sleep almost at once.
"Leon," I enquired, "Are you itching, mate?"
"Yeah, a bit," he replied, and neither able to, nor caring to find out why, went straight to sleep.

The next morning at around 6.00 a.m., I came out of slumber still scratching. I reached into my bag and pulled out a handful of cake, cherries and cream, all mashed together in my bag and on most of my legs, arms and chest. I think our little friends had left a little bedtime snack for us: very sweet and thoughtful.

CHAPTER 3

BACK TO THE 60S WITH DONOVAN CATCHING THE WIND

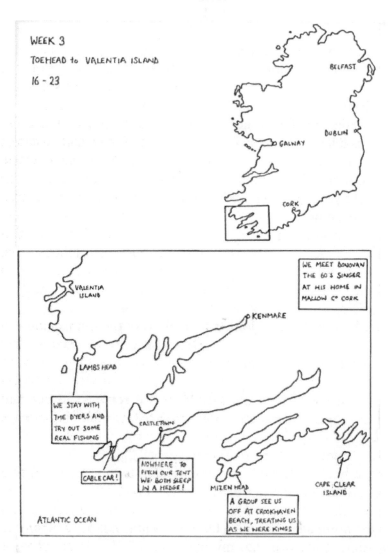

WEEK 3

TOEHEAD to VALENTIA ISLAND

16 - 23

BELFAST

DUBLIN

GALWAY

CORK

VALENTIA ISLAND

WE MEET DONOVAN THE 60'S SINGER AT HIS HOME IN MALLOW C° CORK

KENMARE

LAMBS HEAD

WE STAY WITH THE DYERS AND TRY OUT SOME REAL FISHING

CASTLETOWN

CABLE CAR!

NOWHERE TO PITCH OUR TENT WE BOTH SLEEP IN A HEDGE!

MIZEN HEAD

CAPE CLEAR ISLAND

A GROUP SEE US OFF AT CROOKHAVEN BEACH, TREATING US AS WE WERE KINGS

ATLANTIC OCEAN

Saturday 16th July

Toe Head Bay to Cape Clear to Crook Haven. Distance: 20 miles. Duration: 7 hours. Sea state: calm. Weather: F1 - 2. Sunny and warm, overcast at times.

At 8.30ish our young Irish friend visited. She woke us up with the predicted weather forecast. We rose and fell into what had become an ordered regime of kit packing and dressing. We both knew, without saying, who packed what and in what order. It was now our morning ritual. As neither of us had the inclination to pull out the stove and cook up some porridge - probably because such a conquest would interrupt the routine and both couldn't really be arsed - we instead shared the rest of the Bourbon biscuits; two each. No Irish fry-up today, unfortunately - no invitations had arisen from the lady in the house the night before. The paddling today was hard work. I found my mind wandering and my eyes closing for extended periods of time. I opened them only when I collided with something, or when I'd fallen asleep and my slumping head woke me. It was a very odd experience to be relaxed and tired enough to sleep, but yet still paddling along.

We both knew it was foolish to start a physically-demanding day on practically nothing, because one soon runs out of energy. But cooking up food on a stove and billycans was such a pain in the arse. It took a good hour and a half at least - time we would prefer to save and spend warming ourselves over an open fire engrossed in conversation with the next group of people we might meet.

Hungry and excited, we landed on Cape Clear Island. It looked a little quiet - not unusual for an island. Although we'd been told, along the way, that the cape was a most cherished, lively and tranquil part of the Emerald Isle. Leon and I walked up from the steep jetty, along a grass and stone road, to be greeted by the sight of four blue and pink cottages dotted around the green landscape. Approaching one, I was greeted by a thin man with white wispy hair, red arms and a protruding belly. As he spoke, his black and white Collie yacked, and his petrol lawn mower buzzed and revved. I could barely hear him, so mostly nodded and smiled.

"Is there anywhere to get a bite to eat?" I asked in a raised voice, in an attempt to beat the background noises.

"Ah sure, the grass was too long," he replied. "it needed a trim."

Leon butted in: "It's a great lawn, but I'm Hank Marvin (slang for starving). Where's the pub?"

"I might give the front a lick of paint as well," he replied.

Eventually we gave up. Leon cut the lawn and I played with the dog whilst the old boy put the grub on the table - no such thing as a free lunch!

I've never seen so many earwigs as were taking sanctuary in my boat and especially my buoyancy aid. I counted over 60 of them, and needless to say I was still finding them two hours into our paddle. Every so often I'd jump, pull the deck off and send another earwig to a watery grave.

Sunday 17th July
Crookhaven. Distance: 22 miles. Time: 7 hours. Sea state: calm. Weather: F2, southerly. Warm with blue skies.

As the canoeing took more of a front seat in this expedition, it had the inevitable spin-offs of complete exhaustion and no craving for beer or women. It was a blow today when out of all the quiet and untouched beaches in Ireland that the one we pitched our tent, the Dragon, on was the very one chosen for an all-night bash. The Irish don't need an excuse - even, I'm told, if it is pissing down the party continues.

Under normal circumstances I would call this a stroke of good luck. But as seen through the eyes of wild men it was a "piece of toilet". It left us with the dilemma: do we do as the Romans do? In fact, did we have a choice? Or did we party-poop? As with most things on this trip, the decision was that of basic simplicity. We were both too tired to be Romans, and alas fell under the spell of Captain Zzzz.

The music, boozing, singing and dancing kept us both rolling in and out of sleep. At times, we wished we had the strength to join the Romans; at other times, we wished the centurions would call a bloody halt. At about 4.00 a.m. I heard, coming ever closer, giggles and chatter, stumbling towards the Dragon.

"This is mine, I think," came a slurred, muffled, thick Irish voice. "Now, where's the zip?" he continued. I could see his silhouette swaying back and forth. His arm was around a girl. They were both clutching their prized possession, a bottle of spirit, whilst at the same time trying to open the doorway to our tent. It was only a matter of time, I predicted, before their elephant-like co-ordination caused them to fall forwards or backwards. Preferably backwards, as they'd miss us.

"Leon - a pint on it - forward or backwards?" I said in haste.

"Oh, call me an old cynic, but I say forwards."

"Done!" We shook on it and waited. It wasn't a long wait. In fact we'd only parted hands, when they fell backwards with a crash! As we looked out, their silhouette was exactly the same in every detail, just horizontal this time.

It wasn't over yet. A more convincing assault was in progress. He, using both hands, fumbled to find the zip but was not sure which way to pull. She, holding the bottle, waited, her bum perched on a rock. This time, a guide rope got the better of him and down he went. Third time lucky! The zip opened and he beckoned to his girl with a proud half-smile. Then, he bounced back, after hitting the fly sheet.

"Come on Leon," I said, "their need is greater than ours."

"Yeah, I guess."

As they came in the front, we left at the back. The Dragon was certainly being put through its paces on this expedition. Leon found a comfy bush, and I, a sandy dune.

I awoke next morning, feeling remarkably refreshed considering the lack of sleep, to find the two lovebirds still fast asleep in the Dragon, sharing an overcoat for a blanket. I wandered down to the beach, where our boats lay. The carnage of beer cans, bottles and huddled bodies lay strewn about the place. There was a sweet smell, like burnt cake, in the air from the numerous smouldering remains of campfires.

Our boats were just as we'd left them. As I was changing, a passing jogger pulled in and enquired about the boats.

"Ah sure, I do a little bit of this myself. They're very big boats now," he said walking up and down, inspecting them. "Where do you keep all your clothes and tent?" he asked.

I gave him a guided tour of the boats - in fact he was truly amazed with them. He then, out of the blue, offered to buy them both.

"Name your price," he said.

"That's very kind, but I think I'll hang on to mine - it's got a few miles to go yet," I politely declined, but I did take him up on his second offer of breakfast.

He was on a family holiday, camping close by. Arriving at the campsite, we were whisked into another little adventure. The tent was more of a canvas mobile mansion, with more home comforts than most people's homes. His wife and two children greeted us, and by the time we had a mug of coffee in our mitts, we were surrounded by 15 to 20 other campers whom our host had invited to meet us. This reception carried on right through breakfast and onto the beach, where we were waved off into the morning sun heading for Mizen Head. No doubt, our biggest send-off so far.

Mizen Head is notoriously one of the roughest headlands around Ireland: Charles Haughey, the former Irish premier, lost his 42-foot yacht rounding it. Today though, it was flat and calm, with the odd ripple to prove it wasn't glass. We met some divers going under to look at a ship that went down in 1907 carrying a mixed cargo of pit props, wax and other merchandise.

The day's paddling was enhanced by spectacular close-ups of the rugged coastline. The white tips of the sea rushing in and out of cracks and gullies was mesmerising, just as when one looks into an open fire. All day the air was warm and the sun beamed down. It was a far cry from yesterday's mood. A full belly in the morning makes a huge difference to the day. We stopped only once for lunch on a group of rocks. Here, after much bread and cheese, we snoozed under the warm sun and sounds of the sea.

We eventually stopped for the day at 7.30 p.m. The sun was setting on an idyllic blue and orange sky. The tide guided us into a lonely harbour, with no more than five boats in her. The backdrop was of hills covered in green fields and pine trees. Sea kayaking, for me, didn't get much better than this.

Monday 18th July
Lehanbeg, near Castletown. Sea state: calm/choppy. Weather: F2, dull and drizzly, dark and overcast.

We awoke in Castletown - the closest town to our picturesque harbour where we'd left our boats, 15 miles away. We'd spent the night in a ditch huddled up in a binliner. We'd ended up in this predicament through the usual lack of thought, expecting to chance our way in somewhere.

It all began the night before, when we were approached by two young lads as we pulled our boats up. Leon asked where the nearest town was, and they replied:
"Ah well, dat's Castletown, 15 miles away. We'll give ye a ride, if you're quick." We were very quick. The thought of a warm pub and hot food completely overtook any logical thoughts like: how will we get back? Or will our kit be safe? And where will we sleep? These only came into focus once we'd eaten, and by this stage the stable door had been open a long time.

After trying in vain to hitch back we gave up. We found two binbags, a comfy ditch (if there is such a thing) and went to sleep. Waking with the sun is quite uplifting, even if your legs are numb and pointing out of the bottom of a bin bag, your hairs matted with soil, and your body is uncontrollably shivering with cold. Anyway our dilemma was to get back to our craft, and hitching a lift was our only option.

Now hitching lifts is a precarious game and some dos and don'ts need to be applied:

(i)   Do smile and look normal when you hitch, even if you haven't bathed for a month;

(ii)   Stand in a spot easily seen and easy for a car to stop; try not to put your life in danger, i.e. no hairpin bends.

(iii)   Know where you are going.

(iv)   Chat to the driver.

All were in place apart from number iii). We'd forgotten where we'd landed. So to find out we asked the postman, who conferred with the bread man, who in turn asked the meat man and eventually they told us where we needed to go. And after two hours we eventually set off, and after another two hours and three lifts we ended up at our boats happy and quite tired out.

We'd been invited to stay at the family holiday home of a boy I teach back at Eton. It was 12 miles away, which may not sound a lot on a normal day. Today however, I didn't feel it was a normal day. The weather had changed to gloomy drizzle and we were both feeling in need of a day's rest. I think we were both nearing exhaustion and, even worse, getting fed up with each other's company. Leon didn't say a word from when he got up to when we stopped for lunch. I might as well have been paddling on my own. The silence I found soul-destroying. If you can image two dots in the middle of the ocean relying on each other morally, physically and for motivation, it felt like Leon was failing me on all three counts which was pissing me off. There was a definite conflict looming. I was sure he was just as pissed at me. I would be glad when it happened to clear the air.

Shortly after lunch, I asked Leon where we were and how far did we have to go. Not an unreasonable question, I thought, as he had the nautical chart on his boat. This lit the blue touchpaper. At first Leon ignored me, which really fucked me off.

"Leon, how far?" I repeated.

"I don't know," he replied, evading me.

"You've got the chart."

"Oh, for fuck's sake, I can't paddle and read it," he retorted.

"Well fucking stop then, you arrogant prat." The confrontation had arrived.

"Alright, if you're so keen to navigate, here's the fucking chart!" he shouted, throwing it behind.

"Are little baby's toys coming out of the pram? Where's diddum to spoil you?" I teased, as if addressing a small child. I picked up the map and shook it purposefully, to underline the point. Leon had stopped and was waiting and watching me. I caught up with him.

"Sorry Cathal," he said. "I'm so fucked off with this canoeing. I'm shattered and hungry."

"Yeah, me too. It's great to clear the air though. At least you're talking now."

We continued to chat for the rest of the day, lifting each other's spirits, our symbiotic friendship renewed.

One of the most unexpected and unrivalled sights I've seen in Ireland was en route today, as we passed Dursey Island. The island is linked to the mainland by a blue and yellow cable car, something you might expect to see on a ski resort or in a James Bond film. Dursey is green with a carpet covering of purple and blue heather. It has a mystical bleak appearance, even with its cable car.

As we manoeuvred through its sound, a sailing ship overtook us. Its crew waved and we saw them slowly disappear out to sea. We hugged the rugged coast until we could see Lambs Head, our destination opposite. Before setting off on the two- to three-mile open sea crossing, we stopped to rest and eat. As we bobbed up and down holding each other's kayaks to form a raft, Leon pointed into the distance. I looked, and as they came into view, saw two dolphins jumping in and out of the water playing as they swam along.

Arriving on Lambs Head, a light breeze blowing, our timing was perfect. Our host James, and his two sons Magnus and Crispin, were on the quayside gutting their catch, after an afternoon's fishing. They greeted us and helped to carry our boats up. Their house was a typical-style Irish cottage on the outside, all white-washed and gleaming. The inside was more like a Tardis with its numerous rooms. Its central attraction was the minstrels' gallery.

Tuesday 19th July
Day Off

Tea and coffee have become a big-time luxury on this trip, so to wake up to a piping hot cuppa (even if it was at 7.30 a.m.) was a real treat. Both Leon and I were in the same room. Whilst sipping our tea, we debated whether to have a day off - as it was five days and 76 miles since our last one - or continue. Still not sure, we sat down for breakfast.
"Would you like to stay another night or two? You both look washed out," Carol, James's wife, enquired. I looked at Leon, he at me.
"We'd love to," I said. Leon nodded in agreement and appreciation.

It would seem even on our days off, we'd end up at sea. James had asked if Leon and I fancied a spot of fishing. Neither of us had fished at sea before, so we jumped at this opportunity. I had, after watching the boys gut and clean their catch the day before become almost infatuated by this, and wanted to learn how to do it.

Once out of the bay, we cast our lines with numerous hooks dancing like flies. It was literally only a few seconds before James and Leon had a bite. Two mackerel and a 10 pound pollack, apparently a bland-tasting fish were netted. Then, it was my turn. I felt something on my line and shouted: "I've got one." Just as I shouted, Magnus did. "So have I. Oh, it's a big one!"
We reeled and played our respective big beauties back and forth. James seemed to be looking at me rather oddly, with a kind of knowing grin on his face. The penny dropped: I'd caught Magnus's line!

Back on the quay I was given a lesson in gutting and cleaning, a bit like being a surgeon or butcher.

The post-mistress - Mrs Be-Jesus as she's known - informed me later that day: "Ah, be-Jesus, the man doesn't know the value of the pollock. Sure, be-Jesus, he uses it to bait his lobster pots. I'd cook up a lovely little pollock pie, for us all to feast on. Now, be-Jesus, be sure and tell him I said that, now, won't ye?"

Wednesday 20th July
Lambs Head to Valentia Island. Distance: 18 - 20 miles. Duration: 6 hours. Sea state: very choppy/rough. Weather: F3 - 4, dull and foggy.

This was, I felt, one of the hardest days yet - both mentally and physically. The sea was rough, and wind blowing at Force 4. I would liken it to running the 100-yard dash in a Jacuzzi filled with porridge up to your hips - slow, slippery, hard work and frustrating. It's amazing how many mood swings you can go through in a day's paddle: the hunger pangs, the boredom, the fright, the exhilaration and the anger all interchanging it would seem uncontrollably.

Yesterday my mind was so distant from kayaking I completely switched off, enjoying the Dyers' company and hospitality; also our friend Cathy's. Our friend had flown over from England to see us both. Today, my mind was still distant. This was perhaps the result of the milder seas and weather over the last few days. I think I'd put the rougher seas we'd been through at the back of my mind, perhaps naively hoping I would not have to endure such turbulent water again.

As we left the shelter of the harbour, the turbulent seas and limited foggy vision began to frighten me almost immediately. I began doubting in my ability. My hands were aching as I gripped the paddle shaft too tightly. I was perspiring continuously, my stomach was in ribbons. Rather than thinking coherently, I was panicking; sometimes almost in tears. I was reliving fears and anxieties I should at this stage have been in complete control of. This lack of control was most definitely a negative state of mind and was potentially very dangerous. I really needed to have a clear focus on my paddling.

As time went by at sea, my fears did lessen but I was still not in full control. The exaggerated mood swings were so frequent.

This too was taking its toll. I had never experienced this type of continued panic and lack of self-belief before.

After four hours and much searching, we landed in pouring rain and wind. Both tired and ravenous, we ate without conversation, bread, jam and sardines. Like two half-starved animals, until we could not eat any more. It was at times like this that I so heavily relied on Leon for his support and encouragement. He knew by this stage, I was struggling. A feeling he too had gone through on this trip, and I hope I'd been there to carry the extra burden for him, as he was about to do for me. Both shivering, we tried to warm ourselves by jogging up and down the slipway. Chattering to lift our spirits, knowing we had to continue and make it to Valentia Island, at least another hour and a half away.
"Leon, I don't want to go on. I'm tired and cold, let's call it a day," I pleaded.
"No, come on, you can make it. We'll just blast it to Valentia. There's no point in stopping now," Leon replied and continued: "I know you're not into it today, but you've got to get back in the boat." I knew I had to for if I let it beat me today, it would win every day. A little warmer now, we jumped back into our canoes and set out towards Valentia Island.

A fishing trawler waved us down, concerned at our struggling craft in this water. The fisherman pointed to an uncharted channel obscured by standing waves, with a rock face protecting its entry. Once in this channel, it felt like we were shooting the Zambezi River in monsoon season. High cliffs offering no escape, we had to stay upright for I feared the outcome if we had not. Almost from nowhere, shrouded in fog, Leon spotted Valentia Island.

Both now very excited, we pulled our boats up. Not even changing, I found myself leading Leon, running about and shouting like two excited children, I guess relieving ourselves of this boundless tense energy. Only 20 minutes passed, and we were sitting in safety round an open fire eating cake and tea, another day over, a few miles further.

Later we met up with Cathy. She had, as a treat, brought a guitar. How she found us, I don't know as our directions have been quite sketchy.

Thursday 21st July
Day Off. *Sea state: calm slight swell. Weather: F1-2.*

The first song I'd learnt to play on guitar was the Donovan classic, Catch the Wind. Whilst having a haircut, last year, the owner of the barbershop started talking about Donovan and how he now lived in Ireland. A bit of a long shot, but I phoned his manager in England and enquired if Leon and I might meet and jam with the folk legend whilst on this expedition. I was given the usual: "He's a busy man, but he may be available". To cut a long story short, after numerous faxes, letters and telephone calls, Donovan had agreed to meet up with us. It was now a case of when.

Over breakfast, we discussed trying to meet him today. Leon and I were keen to have a day off and make the most of Cathy's company and, of course, the car! After phoning Donovan's personal assistant, Carol, the night before we were told that Donovan was off to the United States on Friday 22nd to record a new album. It seemed that if we were going to meet him, it was now or never. This left Leon and I faced with a dilemma, not for the first time on this trip. Whether to try and see him by driving two-and-a-half hours to Cork with a slight chance, or, as the weather and sea state were both excellent, to push on to Dingle Bay. The only thing for it was to grab a coffee or two, and try to work it out (or not, as the case may be).

After airing our dilemma with the Skellig's Irish Tourist Board on Valentia, who hadn't even heard of this legend, they offered their telephone to try and phone Donovan's P.A. again. I did, and eventually after many more cups of tea and phone calls, Carol called us back with the news that Donovan would see us at 6.00 p.m. Very excited and a little nervous, we all three jumped into the car and headed for Cork to meet, and hopefully jam with, our hero.

We arrived at a long driveway leading to a large pink house. The gardens were well-kept and as we came closer we could hear children at play and chimes hanging from the trees, setting a very mellow 60s atmosphere. Donovan greeted us warmly at the door and led us into his house. It was very "olde worlde" in decor, again with a definite 60s influence. There was a mini grand piano in the large hallway, with numerous family photos perched upon it. Donovan was wearing clogs, jeans and a baggy shirt, topped off with his now wavy, mousey-grey hair. We turned left into the drawing room, with its large comfy sofas and glorious open fire. After the introductions, we fetched our guitars from the car and sat in the sun. Donovan appeared with his green guitar, a loveheart carved in its middle, some fizzy water and nibbles. I'm not quite sure what was in the fizzy water or if I was just high on the atmosphere. We sat chatting about his musical career, life and loves, for about two hours. He seemed just as interested in our adventure as we were in his lifestyle. Did you know he taught John Lennon how to fingerpick? He played a few of his numbers like Catch the Wind, Universal Soldier and some Irish ballads to boot. We joined in where we could, and he taught us a new song - Julie. All in all his hospitality and willingness to assuage our ferocious, naive appetites for his and others' music, was boundless. As we left, he was keen to see us when he next came to England and play an informal gig at Eton.

Friday 22nd July
Day Off. *Sea state and weather: didn't bother to look today, we tried to keep away from the sea!*

We parked up in Kilkenny and headed for a music shop. I'd decided after our inspirational chat with Donovan that I'd buy a harmonica and rest: the idea being to teach myself to play as I paddled along in the kayak. Possibly the only harmonica-playing canoeist in the world. Unfortunately on returning from this little outing, Cathy - or her hire car to be precise - had been given a parking ticket of £55. This was a lot, we all thought, until we read the footnote left by the warden. The hire car had no road tax, registration, parking permit and two other things. I couldn't quite make this out. Imagine hiring a car and it lacking tax and so on - laid back to say the least, but then it was Ireland!

The rest of the day was spent loafing about on the Ring of Kerry, enjoying the scenery, atmosphere, and occasional sun snooze.

We returned to Valentia Island later that evening. Leon decided he'd sleep in the car parked outside. Cathy and I went to a bed and breakfast overlooking the harbour. Mick, the local diver, had struck on the idea of a dive centre combined with this bed and breakfast. It was no ordinary combination: as you walked in, a decompression chamber lay immediately in your path. A few steps further, the armchairs were disguised by numerous drysuits, wetsuits and the like. In a corner, lay oxygen bottles and lead weights. The whole place was littered with odd and shiny objects, making it difficult for your eyes to focus long enough on one thing, with so much to see.

Feeling sorry for this wild man canoeist, Mick - although having a full house - offered Leon a bed, free of charge. The next morning as I wandered in to breakfast, there appeared to be a kerfuffle around the decompression chamber. I wandered over for a peep and was surprised to see Leon fast asleep in this chamber. His bare butt cheeks were pressed against the glass porthole and his arm around a small teddy bear. He slept on, cocooned in his chamber. Meanwhile Yanks and Japs, cameras flashing, looked on in amazement at this still life exhibition.

CHAPTER 4

FEAR AND FRUSTRATION. THE LAST KNIGHT OF GLIN CASTLE

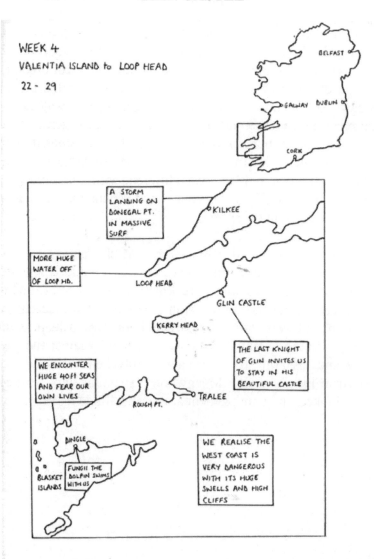

WEEK 4
VALENTIA ISLAND to LOOP HEAD

22 - 29

BELFAST

GALWAY DUBLIN

CORK

A STORM
LANDING ON
DONEGAL PT.
IN MASSIVE
SURF

KILKEE

MORE HUGE
WATER OFF
OF LOOP HD.

LOOP HEAD

GLIN CASTLE

KERRY HEAD

THE LAST KNIGHT
OF GLIN INVITES US
TO STAY IN HIS
BEAUTIFUL CASTLE

WE ENCOUNTER
HUGE 40 ft SEAS
AND FEAR OUR
OWN LIVES

TRALEE

ROUGH PT.

DINGLE

BLASKET
ISLANDS

FUNGH THE
DOLPIN SWIMS
WITH US

WE REALISE THE
WEST COAST IS
VERY DANGEROUS
WITH ITS HUGE
SWELLS AND HIGH
CLIFFS

Saturday 23rd July

Valentia to Dingle. Distance: 17 miles. Duration: 5 hours, Sea state: rough. Weather: F4 south-westerly, dull and rain.

Cathy saw us off at the Valentia bridge as we set out on our longest open crossing so far on the trip, a nine-miler. The wind was blowing at Force 4 from the south-west, which was just what we wanted to help push us along. I felt odd at the thought of being so far from land. Just a small, virtually-invisible, dot in a vast blue sea. It was an odd kind of freedom, knowing nothing could get to me as no-one knew I was there. However, I had the luxury of contacting someone if I wanted. My distress flares were in my bum bag strapped to me. I was moving at a pace I set, doing and controlling exactly what I wanted. There was no interaction with anyone, except of course Leon, but in this scenario he didn't count. For at sea, we were one. Perhaps this is what people mean, when they talk of "true freedom".

The crossing took only two hours, due to the tide and wind's help. It was like a day out at White Sands in Pembrokeshire, surfing along and fooling around. I also had a harmonica hanging around my neck today. It was the Donovan influence upon me. I noticed Leon kept his distance as I tried playing and singing, with little style or rhythm. Luckily for Leon, this expressive apparition of Donovan didn't last. I lost my balance momentarily on the crest of a surf wave, went partially upside down, luckily recovering, only to find my harmonica lost overboard.

We arrived in Dingle Harbour to be greeted by its hermit dolphin, Fungi, splashing and jumping around our boats. I'd expected Fungi to resemble Flippa, from a Saturday morning television show I'd watched as a child - with his slick blue body and white teeth. Fungi, in real life, was much larger than this. He must have been as wide as a small fishing boat and about 25 feet long. An immense creature, we were both, at first, unnerved by this size. His white belly and blue back were polka-dotted by scar tissue, possibly from collisions with motorboat engines and the like. His teeth were white and stained, and his face looked quite weathered - I would say even wrinkled - with age. Not as I'd expected, but still an amazing sight to greet your eyes. He was a major tourist attraction in Dingle, I think he'd become almost the equivalent of the Queen and Windsor Castle in England.

Sunday 24th July
Dingle to Ballyferriter. Distance: 18 miles. Duration: 6 hours. Sea state: choppy large swell (40 ft). Weather: F4 - 5.

We were now a third of the way through this trip. I was now at the stage where I was wondering why I was doing this and how I could justify it. Physically it was exhausting, but we were both coping with that with no real problems, just the odd ache and pain. The mental frustrations and boredom at sea were, at times, grinding me down. Today we got into our boats in Dingle Harbour and sat paddling solidly for six hours, fuelled by one chocolate bar the whole 18 miles.

The day was calm as we waved goodbye to Cathy on the harbour wall for the last time. She was going back to England today. On entering the bay, we paused to watch Fungi the hermit dolphin, splashing and jumping. We left its shelter both knowing we could not exit our boats until Ballyferriter 18 miles away, due to the high cliffs that guarded the land from the Atlantic swell.

The sea was rough. The wind in our faces, and the tide against us, made the first three hours exhilarating but draining. On the approach to Blasket Sound, a small fishing trawler came alongside, warning us of a gale heading our way. We had two choices. We could go back and set out again tomorrow on the same journey, wasting time, energy and morale. Or we could chance it and head to our intended destination. We both decided on the latter. We entered Blasket Sound - its tide of 3 knots was running in our favour. This provoked fear and excitement, a bit like a ride on a roller coaster. The water was fast, white and bubbling, camouflaging numerous rocks in its swell.

On the other side of the peninsula, something we had anticipated but did not want to believe, was the 30 to 40 foot high rolling

Atlantic swell. The sheer size of this water, as seen from our small craft, was most definitely one of my most vivid experiences on this trip. We were without a doubt coping with water that could so easily and so quickly have taken our lives. People say in these situations that they put this fear to the back of their minds - I cannot say I did. The fear and potential danger were vivid and at the forefront of my mind. I accepted the reality of being so close to death and this kept me going.

With three hours still to go, before we might land, it was incredible how this fear lessened and perception changed with time. This huge swell now became normality, and with this rationalization, fear was replaced by monotony. At one stage, relief came in the form of an earwig crawling up my leg, inside the canoe. This irrational feeling, coupled with the insect biting me, gave a perverted relief. I almost enjoyed this interference, as it removed the focus from the monotonous paddling.

Deciding to lift our morale and mood by eating chocolate, I opened my deck, and fumbling around, I eventually came up with two bars. In the meantime, I was so engrossed in my search, I had not noticed that I'd drifted precariously close to rocks with surf breaking over them. With haste I paddled away, only to drop the chocolate, that I so craved, into the sea. The frustration was almost too much. I lifted my paddle and beat the surrounding water screaming and shouting: "Bastard, fucking bastard," only to burst into perverse laughter. The value of that chocolate fix, at that moment, was indescribable.

The wind had definitely started to lift as the gale moved closer. With perhaps half an hour to go, on what seemed a never-ending journey. I spotted a small shingle beach and headed for it. With each painful stroke, the wind only allowed limited headway, although the water was now calmer on entering this bay. I sat in my boat, its front edged on to the beach, trying to digest the day's events. This was only interrupted when I realised I'd become rather cold; my body was uncontrollably shivering. Leon told me afterwards that I'd been sitting motionless, staring ahead for almost 20 minutes. I think I was in a kind of exhausted shock.

Once changed again, as so often on this expedition I forgot about canoeing, my thoughts turned to food and relaxation.

Monday 25th July
Stormbound. Weather: gale force. Sea state: I hate to think!

One of our sponsors, Jack Wolfskin, very kindly gave us a tent called The Dragon. They said it was just the job for our trip: it was shaped like an elongated limpet shell and was incredibly easy to erect, even in wind and rain. Last night, it really proved its worth when in gale force wind and rain we pitched on a hill with no defences - it took a beating, it was bending and lifting all night and yet we were amazed at its durable, ridged but bendy body. Not a drop of rain penetrated the Dragon's defences.

I awoke at around 9.00 a.m. The gale was still very persistent and now had united with thick fog, giving an early feel to our surroundings. It didn't take us long to conclude that canoeing today was most definitely off. Inside the tent, the atmosphere was that of a damp, rancid sock. Everything - clothes, sleeping bags and even us - had a layer of thin, smeggy dew on it. I craved for a warm, sweet atmosphere to replace this. Even with rain lashing, I insisted we find refuge elsewhere. After pegging the tent down, hoping it would stay, we set off into the village, four miles away - a pleasant walk on a sunny day, but a nightmare in this weather. Yesterday, with Cathy, regrettably I decided to send back my waterproofs to lessen the load. Leon had not, so today he was warm, happy and dry; whereas I was wet, cold and pissed off. It's always the same: whatever you don't pack, you end up needing the most. Not all was bad luck though. Due to my drowned-rat appearance, a kind lady took pity on me, exchanging my sodden trousers and top for her husband's similar dry clobber. She then told me to return in an hour or so, when they'd be clean and dry. Where else but in Ireland would one receive such kindness? Refreshed and warm, we headed to the coffee shops, museums, and any other dry haven, Ballyferriter had to offer.

Later that same afternoon, I found myself in need of peace and tranquillity. This, I found oddly enough, in a church. There was a high wall surrounding the church and its graveyard - possibly through boredom, I found myself balancing and walking along it. I ventured further into the graveyard and finally into the church itself. I sat on an old wooden pew in complete warm, motionless silence. The contrast between this and the previous day, I found comforting and safe. Here I stayed, in a staring trance, like a battery on charge. The only person to disturb my moments was an old lady. She came in, lit a candle, knelt in prayer, acknowledged me with a smile and left. It was refreshing to get away from Leon: a healthy change, my own space.

Most of our day was spent in the two coffee shops, flitting from one to the other to change the scene. After the paper had been read from cover to cover, posties had been written and sent, girlfriends and mums phoned, boredom began to set in.

The Dingle peninsula is windswept, but not barren by any means. It is true to say it is geared to the tourist, with every other house a bed and breakfast, and every other bed and breakfast a pub. The people in the area still live as, and indeed are, a community. It was a community very used to the tourist, and very accommodating and friendly to him or her. The scenery on land or at sea was, as most of Ireland, green and breath-taking. Dingle was the setting for the big Tom Cruise blockbuster "Far and Away". In fact, the hotel he and the cast stayed in is full of "Far and Away" memorabilia, even a signed portrait of Tom himself.

Eventually at around 3.00 p.m., we hit the village pub with its traditional live music. Both the food and the welcomes were very warm: a recommended stop-off. Two of the girls heard of our predicament and feeling rather sorry for us (especially me dressed in someone else's clothes) decided to pack us into their battered motor and give us a guided tour of Dingle. Up mountain and down dale, we were shown every nook and cranny, until like two tired babies we fell asleep in the back of the car.

Tuesday 26th July
Ballyferriter to Rough Point. Distance: 18 miles. Duration: 4/5 hours. Weather: sea state rough and some swell.

I sat looking out at the bleak coast and scenery, eating a bag of cheese and onion crisps and a lump of stale cake. A rather odd breakfast mix, but I kept telling myself: it's only fuel. I don't think I even tasted it. The wind had dropped and the sun was just making a faint appearance in the sky, although not shining.

After that last day at sea I was still nervous, in fact shit-scared. My hands were shaking and I felt like going to the loo, even though I'd just been. Leon and I didn't say a word. I had to force myself into the boat. I really didn't want to go on. Once afloat, this feeling got worse. I was gripping my paddle so tightly my knuckles were white; I was perspiring and still shaking. It was Valentia all over again. I felt so het-up I could hardly balance upright in my boat. Still neither of us spoke. In front, I could see the harbour opening and the rough white tails of the sea beyond. I was, at this point, almost in tears. The fear and anxiety were destroying my ability to concentrate or think clearly. I had to pull myself together. Concentrating on my paddle blade cutting in and out of the water, I began to slowly relax. My stomach stopped churning. Slowly, my confidence returned - never fully though; just enough to keep me going. As the day progressed, so too did the severity of seas, with 20 foot swell, and twice that day confusing standing waves, easily as long as our boats. This water was terrifying. I found it best to look ahead, as looking behind created a much more ferocious picture of water cascading toward one's boat. Somehow, looking ahead did not create such images. I'm glad we did not speak as we launched today, and deep down I knew why. Leon, too, was unsure and frightened. If we had disclosed our fears, the day would have been even harder and we might not have gone on. But our silence could be taken as a very clear boost to one another, almost competitive: if he can do it so can I. An odd, but symbiotic relationship. At least, after the morning's painful moments, I felt confident and happy, with 18 miles covered when landing today. But more importantly, I was proud of our staying power.

There was however one problem, not directly related to canoeing, that nonetheless did not help matters. It was a hygiene problem: two days earlier our toothpaste supply had run out. By now, my mouth tasted of salty fish. The furry texture of plaque on my teeth was hard to ignore and worse still, halitosis might be setting in. With the increased wild man diet of often many sugary foods it was probably our most important hygiene task, to clean our teeth, for they were taking a beating. Spillane's Bar, half a mile's walk from our landing had some of the cheapest, filling food, I've had in Ireland. It even, oddly enough, sold toothpaste over the bar.

Looking ahead to tomorrow: Gerald FitzGerald, the Knight of Glin, whom I contacted many months earlier telling of our intended voyage, had kindly invited us to supper at Glin Castle. The only problem I foresaw was that it was 30 miles from the coast!

Wednesday 27th July
Rough Point to River Shannon. Distance: 11 Miles. Duration: 5 hours. Sea state: rough, 15-20 foot swell and breaking waves. Weather: F3 and cold.

As Kerry Head came into view about three miles ahead, so too did the mouth of the River Shannon. We expected turbulent water because: firstly, a headland is always choppy; and secondly, a river emptying is bound to be rivalled by a jealous sea. Not what I'd call cricket, what! And indeed, this combination delivered a googly. The water was spectacular. The breakers were sometimes 20 feet and the overfalls were easily 15. We had planned to cross to the aptly-named Loop Head. But our plan changed as the swell and breaking waves increased in ferocity. So instead, escaping from the battle, we turned tail, heading four miles up the Shannon. For the first two miles, we fought with this torment of the river and sea. It only calmed as we entered a small harbour where we threw in the towel, for that day at least. It seemed odd that children played, swimming and jumping off rocks, in this safe haven - oblivious to the dangers beyond. The line between safety and danger at sea is so finely drawn.

Once changed into dry kit, our thoughts turned from survival to Glin Castle and what awaited us there. Thirty miles to travel, which was at least an hour by car, if we had one - and God knows how long by 'hitcher's thumb'. I noticed I was soon out of breath walking up the steep, sharp, hill from the harbour. My spindly muscle-barren legs creaked beneath me. They were mostly redundant on this trip, locked in a canoe, wasting away. The topic of our conversation was the Lotto - Ireland's National Lottery - this week's pot was two and a half million.
"How would you spend it Leon?" I enquired.
"I'd hire a cab to Glin Castle... No, with two and a half million, I'd buy one!" came the reply.
Soon after, came our first lift - a large, red-haired man who had just visited England for the first time. He was obviously fascinated by Windsor Safari Park.
"Ye fellas live in Windsor, and you've never been to see the lions and monkeys? Are ye frightened? Sure they're all in big bar sheds - they can't get out," he explained, insisting we go when we got back. After eight miles or so, we were back on Shanks's pony. We walked and walked and walked for three hours without a sniff of a lift or even a passing car. Eventually at 7.30 p.m., enough was enough. Bored and knackered I decided to chance my arm, knocking on a door; a bit like "cold calling" except this was "cold hitching". Mike O'Connor of Kilgarvan answered the door, delighted with our "neck" (an Irish colloquial meaning "nerve"). He gave us the half-hour lift to Glin Castle and asked only a postcard to let him know how the night at the castle turned out. Neither of us had stayed in a castle before and had not been offered yet. But we felt the knight might take pity on the wild men we certainly looked, and we probably smelled in need of good hospitality.

On arrival at Glin Castle we were shown into the smoking room by Dedra, the housekeeper. We walked through the main hall - it was the size of half a football pitch - and I was impressed by its splendour. The coving around the ceiling was so exact: the ceiling was painted with an elaborate lady in a blood-red cape relaxing on a chaise longue. In the centre, hung a massive chandelier. The walls were covered in hung portraits of previous knights of Glin Castle. The hall boasted ornate tables and chairs. On one of the tables, the visitors' book lay open. It had guests listed from many parts of the world including: the U.S.A., England and Hong Kong. A small piano grandly stuck out from the left-hand corner, which Leon tinkled on for a few minutes.

The smoking room was of similar décor, with more recent family portraits and photographs. The best part for me was the roaring log fire surrounded by comfy, user-friendly sofas and armchairs, onto one of which I flopped. On the coffee table lay a selection of magazines: mainly House & Home, or House & Garden, with the occasional Hello magazine in between. On closer inspection, most of the magazines contained articles on Glin Castle or its occupants.

The double doors opened and the Knight of Glin, Gerald FitzGerald, entered. He introduced himself with a big smile.
"Would you fellows like a drink of something?" he offered.
"We've just ordered a cup of tea," I said.
"I'm sure you could manage something stronger," he insisted. "An Irish perhaps, as you've canoed all day."
"I'd love a beer," Leon said.
"Beer would be great," I seconded.
"Beer it is then," the Knight said triumphantly, in a very proper English accent.
"Well now, as you have a beer to keep you going, shall I show you both around?"
So off on a Cook's tour of Glin Castle, through house and garden - including a working kitchen garden where all the vegetables, flowers and so on, were grown for the castle itself.

The Knight enquired as to how we'd travelled to Glin.
"Good Lord, it took six hours to hitch!" he exclaimed. "Where will you stay tonight?"
"I guess some ditch, or under a tree, on the way back," Leon answered, a wry smile on his face.
"No, no, you must stay here for the night and I'll have Dedra

drive you back in the morning."

Of course, we'd hoped this might happen and accepted his kind offer like a beggar man snatching a five pound note. I later discovered that select guests pay £110 a night to stay in the castle.

Supper was a sharp contrast to our usual style of pie and pint. Instead, we sat under candlelight, in the very plush dining room. Each plate was surrounded by a Mensa Test of cutlery, with a bottle of red wine breathing in the middle of the mahogany table. The Knight and his guests were dressed for dinner, and allowed our shabby wild appearance to go unspoken and apparently unnoticed. It was almost like going back in time or being on the set of a B.B.C. period costume drama. The food was not the usual wild man tucker, and for a change I even tasted it. I did, however, stumble on the artichoke starter. I've never eaten artichoke before, so I watched to see how it was done, then copied. All was fine, dipping and eating in turn each of the 50 or so leaves, even if it was a little tedious. Then came the actual heart. Feeling confident, I decided to take my own lead. I cut a chunk, dropped it into my mouth and chewed. It tasted foul, having the texture of a bramble bush. I uncontrollably coughed, and out it flew, landing just beside the candelabra. The conversation stopped and all eyes were focused on me. I politely smiled and picked up the "fall-out", in my napkin. Leon looked over, a big grin on his face. "Marvellous artichokes - the best I've ever had!" I said confidently, hoping to be forgiven my faux pas.

"Yes, yes, marvellous," the Knight seconded and his guests echoed.

Our bedroom was in the style of the rest of the castle - elaborate and classic. The shower was a welcome wash down.

Thursday 28th July

River Shannon to Ross Point Bay. Distance: 16 miles. Time: 4 hours. Sea state: choppy/rough swell. Weather: south-west wind, F2 - 3, moderate.

Dedra, as promised, dropped us back to reality - if indeed trying

70

to canoe around Ireland can be considered reality. Today's objective was to round Loop Head; anything else was a bonus. A local, standing watching us, told us: "You'll round her or drown in the waters that surround her." A comforting thought to start the day! The Shannon, running in our favour, took us very quickly to the Loop. It's called the Loop because the seabed beneath it does just that. It loops, causing turbulent looping surf and swell. If this wasn't enough, the Shannon emptying exaggerates and adds to the turmoil.

We were committed to fast-moving, heavy-rolling surf, moving without pattern or continuity. Staying close together in this exhilarating and terrifying water, we watched each other being uncontrollably tossed about by the cutting and elaborate water. A capsize in this would have been very tricky, if not terminal. The tidal stream was taking us in the favoured direction. All I had to concentrate on was keeping my craft upright and away from rocks. It was one of the roughest seas yet encountered.

It seemed ironic after the day's events on the Loop that later in the evening we met one of the local helicopter rescue pilots, Paul Husband. He filled us in on all the rescues off Loop Head over the years, bringing a chill to our bones.

Friday 29th July
Ross Point Bay to Donegal Point. Distance: 12 miles. Sea state: choppy with swell; then gale-force storm landing. Weather: F2 - 3, S.W. gusting F6.

Whilst I packed kit into my canoe this morning, I could just see the outlines of two figures approaching. As they came into view, I noticed an adult walking with a limp and a tot held tightly by the hand
"Will ye abandon?" asked Paddy, in a thick Irish voice.
"No, I think we'll give it a go," I answered.
"God, you're courageous men. Sure I wouldn't go out in that swell!" he declared and in the same breath continued, "Would ye fellers take a cup of tea, before ye go? It might be your last!" He gave a big smile.

"We would," I said.

We both followed Paddy and his grandson, Mark, back over the field up the mud track to his farmhouse. Inside I sat by the range - which warmed the kitchen and kettle - tucking into bread, butter and jam, slugging down gulps of tea in between our conversation.

The swell was still up, but not as bad as yesterday. After about two-and-a-half hours, the wind started to increase until it was gusting around gale force, trying to blow us off the shore and seaward. The high cliffs offered some shelter, but in this wind not enough. We tried to make a hasty retreat, but the wind's strength was almost too much. It took us almost an hour to travel one mile to the shore. Our dilemma, now, was how and where to land. The only available option was on a sloping, rocky shore with large surf dumping on it. Dumping surf and rock to a fibreglass kayak is like a flyswat to a small mouse. Depending on where and how hard you swat the mouse will determine the damage, so we needed to time our landing with the smaller surf. To try and control the landing, we had a plan. Leon held the boats together while I pulled off my spray deck (a spray deck keeps water from entering the cockpit) and turned sideways on, with my legs hanging over the edge into the sea. The idea was to jump out at the appropriate moment and guide the raft home, lessening any damage.

The landing started well: whilst sitting on the raft we both surfed in until almost on the rocks, then I jumped off intending to guide the raft home. Unfortunately, as with most things on this trip, it wasn't quite this simple. My foot caught in the kayak guide rope and like a bumbling fool I found myself upside down, still attached to an out-of-control kayak. Leon lost the raft and it turned over; all the kit stowed in the cockpit (luckily mostly tied in) floated free in the surf. We both picked ourselves up, laughing I think with fright, and scrambled with the boats, paddles and kit, trying to drag it ashore. Surf was now breaking all over us. We both kept slipping and falling on algae but eventually retrieved almost everything except the very precious £1,500 film camera, which was looping the loop in the surf. Like two Pit bull terriers at lunchtime, we dived back into the surf and pulled it ashore - fortunately it was shaken but not stirred. Our little plan had vaguely worked. The only thing to suffer, apart from ego and drenched equipment, were my knees and Leon's elbow grated like cheese on the barnacles. Blood poured from them; however these were exaggerated injuries, nothing serious. For the last couple of years, Leon had been suffering with a hernia. It generally didn't cause any problems, but over the last week it had started to twinge a little, especially today, after the precarious landing. He had a definite limp and dull pain when walking. I hoped it would die down again.

We left our craft pulled on to the grassy verge and walked over fields to nearby Doonbeg. I asked on reaching the local grocery shop as to where we might find a cup of tea and food, only to be shown into their kitchen where we received ham sandwiches and tea in exchange for details of our journey. Again, only in Ireland, eh!

The forecast for the next day was for southerly gales - just what we could do without!

CHAPTER 5

BREATHTAKING CONNEMARA, MAD COWS AND RAIN

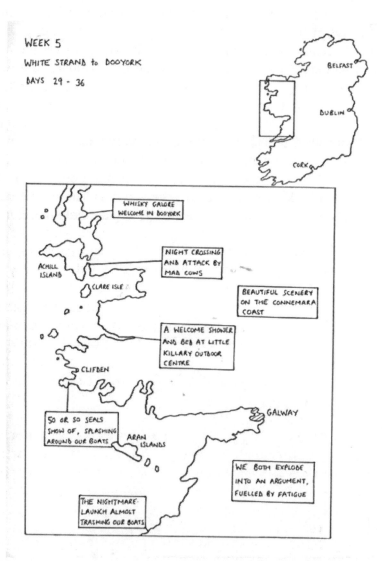

WEEK 5

WHITE STRAND to DOOYORK

DAYS 29 - 36

BELFAST

DUBLIN

CORK

WHISKY GALORE WELCOME IN DOOYORK

NIGHT CROSSING AND ATTACK BY MAD COWS

ACHILL ISLAND

CLARE ISLE

BEAUTIFUL SCENERY ON THE CONNEMARA COAST

A WELCOME SHOWER AND BED AT LITTLE KILLARY OUTDOOR CENTRE

CLIFDEN

GALWAY

50 OR SO SEALS SHOW OF, SPLASHING AROUND OUR BOATS

ARAN ISLANDS

WE BOTH EXPLODE INTO AN ARGUMENT, FUELLED BY FATIGUE

THE NIGHTMARE LAUNCH ALMOST TRASHING OUR BOATS

Saturday 30th July
White Strand to Mutton Island to Dous. Distance: 20 miles. Weather: F3, south-westerly.

The day began with us almost trashing the expedition boats. Still stranded on sloping rocks enclosed by sweeping and dumping six- to eight-foot surf, our dilemma was to try and launch into this washing machine of saltwater or carry the laden boats about half a mile up a very steep, wet and slippery, green and brown hill, covered in barbed wire obstacles. On the other side of this mound lay a sheltered pool, dropping into the sea; an ideal spot to launch, but we decided almost impossible to get to.

We opted for the former and sheepishly set up our boats ready to go. The surf was breaking and sweeping strongly to the left. This made it tricky to head straight into the breaking wave; this backwash may have pulled the boats sideways making a launch impossible, or even worse, trashing you and the kayak on the rocks beneath.

We both knew how to launch into surf: you face up and speed-paddle like stink directly at the breaking wave, trying to burst through. It must be accurate. If your boat is not at 90 degrees to the incoming wave, it can take control of you and the boat. The outcome is quite uncertain, a bit like a car accident. You may be totally unhurt, or well, who knows?

Leon and I were both very nervous. Sheepishly setting our boats down, we watched and studied the breakers for 10 minutes or so, deciding they briefly calmed to 3 - 4 feet, about every 20 wave cycles. This was the only time to launch. Even more nervous now, we tried to psyche ourselves up by beating our chests and shouting. Then, quiet. The moment had arrived. We would go together, believing safety in numbers was best. Neither wished to make the sacrifice of launching the other.

We edged closer, the surf's backwash was still sweeping strongly to the left, creating confused water. This launch was going to test our skill, nerve and luck. We climbed hesitantly into our kayaks just beyond the reach of the backwash. I had my spray deck on, Leon was still fumbling with his, when the tail-end of the wash caught his boat causing premature take-off. The boat, which moments before was next to mine, was now heading sideways into seven foot high breaking surf. Leon was bracing his arm against the jagged rock, as he raced into boiling white water.

I had no choice but to shove off and follow. When I reached him, he had somehow retrieved his paddle. This was only the first part of his good fortune: his second was when my boat hit his head on, and by sheer luck he ended up in a perfect position so that all he needed to do was paddle. By the same token, however, I was now side on. As Leon paddled to safety and freedom, I could see a 'mother' of a breaker coming in. I tried in vain to fight the wash and straighten my laden harness. No good - it hit me with ferocious force, lifting, tossing, and dumping me; its strong backwash like a long arm clawing me back.

I braced myself against it with my paddle and hung on. It carried me about 20 feet, then threw me upside down onto the rocks. "Jesus Christ, are you okay?" I heard Leon shout. I tried to look up, but in vain. Another, and then another breaker, smashed down on the boat. I knew all I could do was wait until it calmed, then jump out of the kayak and pull it up out of the surf. It's not easy to stay composed though when large breakers keep forcing you under. It calmed for a brief moment and I was out of my kayak, belly down, and scrambling to my feet still holding my kayak and paddle. The tail-ends of the breakers knocked me over a few times, but eventually I made it to safety.

I was shaking uncontrollably and bleeding from my legs and arms. I had no choice but to try again. I could just see Leon, keeping his position just past the point where the waves were breaking, about 200 yards away. The noise of wind and surf made it impossible to communicate, I felt totally alone. Two more attempts were made, with similar outcome. The boat was taking a beating. If this were to continue, it might finish the expedition. I was frustrated and annoyed; why couldn't I be sitting where Leon was? With hindsight, my next move was bold to say the least. I put all mine and Leon's apples in one cart, so to speak. I felt my only option was to launch the boat empty and hope Leon could get to it. I'd then try to swim through and under the surf.

I shouted to Leon, knowing he wouldn't hear me, but it felt reassuring: "Leon, I'm launching the boat, get the towline on it." Then I went for it, running full pelt at the surf forcing the boat through. "The boat! Get the fucking boat!" I screamed. It hadn't quite made safe water and was being carried sideways onto the rocks. I was now in deep water, clinging to my paddle and swimming through incoming surf, swallowing most of it. I could just see snippets of Leon; he was next to my boat appearing to push it. It transpired afterwards that his towline was not to hand, so he had instead used his fishing line to tow my craft to safety.

It was a good 10 minutes before Leon and I were reunited. I was quite exhausted swimming in such cold water.

The boat was, as you might expect, full of water. But we had no time to empty it, so Leon helped me in and I paddled what now resembled a wobbling floating fish tank. We were both perversely laughing aloud, nervously relieved to be reunited. Once in safer water, Leon emptied my boat as I dangled over the side. A lucky escape!

Our whole epic launch from start to finish lasted 55 minutes. I later noticed I'd lost the compass from the front of my kayak in all the confusion and there was also a small hole in my hull.

Both starving, we only managed to paddle for about an hour or so, stopping on Mutton Island. It was dull drizzle that welcomed us. We sat shivering, not talking, but eating and eating the remains of yesterday's supper: bread, rice pudding, beans and salad cream. I think we were suffering a kind of delayed shock.

As the day progressed, we passed under the 900-foot cliffs of the Moher. They gave us shelter from the prevailing wind. The swell seemed to disappear; the sun setting gave the cliffs an almost magical presence. We moved along in a kind of timeless limbo.

We arrived on the Doolin slipway just as ferry left to take passengers to the now very popular Aran Islands. I say now, for only in the last eight years or so have they become tourist spots. Before then, they were struggling to survive. There are three Aran Islands: Inisheer, Inishmaan and Inishmore. All are barren, covered in handmade stone walls built over decades, to protect land and livestock from the elements. I was on the Aran Islands five years ago, and even since then it had undergone much change. Now a commercialised expensive place, losing its character to commercial greed - not a place I would recommend for a visit.

Sunday 31st July
Doolin, Co. Clare to Aran Islands to Gorumna, Co. Galway. Distance: 21 miles. Duration: 7 hours. Sea state: calm. Weather: F6 dropping to F3 in afternoon.

Starting late to avoid the predicted bad weather, fog and southerly Force 6 winds, was always a favourite – we enjoyed the excuse for an extended sleep. We landed on each Aran Island in turn. All were very lively due to the bank holiday weekend. On the biggest, Inisheer, we persuaded the young lady running the hostel to let us grab a shower. She agreed immediately, suggesting that a haircut and shave would also improve our wild appearance. After a large meal costing a small fortune we wandered around, in and out of the numerous gift shops and sweater-selling cottages. We were caught up like sheep following the one in front in a flock of people: Germans, Yanks and all. I was feeling agitated in this atmosphere. It was a bit like a ski resort without snow, and lacking the sleepy atmosphere of the rest of Ireland. When Leon suggested an evening paddle to the mainland of Galway, I jumped at the suggestion.

This was the first night paddle of the trip. The sun was setting in an orange and purple sky, creating a beautiful masterpiece. The water was flat and calm with an occasional swell, proving it wasn't glass. There was no wind in our warm surroundings. I looked at my watch, which read 8.40 p.m. Gorumna, where we were heading, was an estimated to be two hours away. As we moved off, our mood was that of excited children, doing something new for the first time. We were chattering and laughing, glad to be away from the island. As darkness fell, we were both silent; all that could be heard was the sound of our paddles striking the water in unison. Once in darkness, our sight lost, the sounds of the sea intensified. I was amazed at how loud it all sounded, the light splash of water on rock, magnified to sound like a breaking wave. Still neither of us broke this silence with words. We were feeling confident, comfortable in our own thoughts. Eventually we could just see something shining on the mainland. I would estimate from our vantage point at sea, we would have a naked view of two to three miles of coast. Yet only one light could we see. It was a measure of Ireland's bleakness.

By good fortune, we landed on a tiny slipway surrounded by small boats. It was a cumbersome procedure, slipping and sliding on algae and weeds; fumbling to find dry clothes and the tent. Walking towards our still-distant light, we could just make out a very pot-holey path. We tried, stumbling at times, to follow its curves and bends. The light, as we'd hoped, was a pub still serving at gone midnight.

Monday 1st August
Gorumna Island to Bunowen Bay, Co. Galway. Distance: 20 miles. Duration: 6 - 7 hours. Sea state: calm. Weather: sunny and warm.

Connemara was true sea canoeing country. The topography had completely changed: the high hills and cliffs had all but moved back from the immediate coast, leaving in their wake glorious beaches and rocky shores easily landed upon.

The novelty of being able to pull in and pee at will was getting out of control. In our first hour today, we pulled in and peed 4 times. The real bonus though, was not having to limit fluid consumption. Before, with high cliffs to contend with, stopping was a nightmare if not impossible. More fluid quite often alleviated fatigue and painful headaches. After all, our bodies were losing water, by sweating and continual exposure to wind and sun.

Towards the middle of the day, fog sneaked up on us, eventually smothering land and sea, creating a grey atmosphere and a need to navigate by map and compass. Luckily, Leon still had the latter. Out of this monotonous shroud came two local fishermen in a currach, a small traditional oval-shaped boat, made out of wood and tar. They were both standing hauling up a net, dressed in yellow oilskins, sleeves rolled up and trouser legs tucked into their black wellies. They seemed as surprised to see us, as we were them. At first, they looked at us as if we were a vision or something. I came alongside their currach. "Do you know which way land is? We're a little lost."
"Lost is it? Well if ye go dat way," he said pointing straight, "you'll eventually hit something. Isn't dat right Pat"? He turned to his companion.
"Ahh, aye, well, you might as well go dat way. It's as good as any," he agreed. A lengthy chat followed, enriched by a few sips of warm tea.

Both feeling fairly knackered, we stopped and exited the boats. Again reverting back to wild men, we ate till fit to burst, then ate some more, eventually curling up and falling into a deep siesta.

There were two young seal pups playing and fighting with each other, so involved at play that they didn't see us sneak up on them until we were within about four to five feet. Then, a huge `splash'! They saw us, and they were gone. Seals are a common sight to the sea canoeist; these animals are generally very inquisitive and often follow boats for miles. Alternatively some don't even bat an eyelid, staying put. Close up their face looked a little like that of a large black Labrador: its nose extended, whiskers thickened, nostrils exaggerated, and steam lifting from it. From a distance, all one saw in the water was a bobbing black buoy.

Both of us were keen to watch and see more of our young

companions, so we followed them. They watched us and we them; we were being led back to their nest. Edging around a jagged piece of rock, to our pleasure and surprise we saw 50 to 60 seals. Some were sunbathing, big bellies flopped on the supporting rocks. Others dashed into the water at the sight of our craft. Many swam under and around, surveying us. It was like a nature movie. We had stopped paddling, and were sitting and watching, pointing and shouting at the parade before and around us. Their presence was quite magical. We observed, infatuated by their bobbing heads and explosive splashes. It was meetings like this that gave the expedition meaning and worth, and gave our fatigued bodies the spirit to continue.

Tuesday 2nd August - longest day
Bunowen Bay, Little Killary. Distance: 28 miles. Sea state: calm. Weather: sunny and warm.

Today was one of our longest paddles. Our bodies were weak and ached with fatigue. Our minds, though, were made strong at the thought of getting to Little Killary Adventure Centre. The canoeing fraternity was rather small and friendly and we'd been invited to stay there for the night. This offer meant good food, comfy beds and a shower, which we were much looking forward to. The day was still, at first, with sunny warm skies. We were on the water early and refreshed by a warm cup of tea. After about four-and-a-half hours, we stopped for a rest and lunch. Knowing it would be a slog to get to Little Killary, we didn't want to waste too much time.

The weather took a turn at about 4.00 p.m. The sun disappeared, to be replaced by cloud and hail. The wind then chilled our weary bodies, blowing an irritating Force 3 into our faces, turning our pleasant day into a shitty one. I had reached the point where frustration, fatigue and incredible hunger were beginning to make my mood aggressive and possibly irrational. Leon was probably feeling the same, but as he was saying little, I was not fully aware. His silence was adding to this mood, especially as he had the fucking map. I felt like a blind man being led by an incompetent mute. We'd already paddled down two estuaries at

Leon's navigation. This tiresome incompetence, as I saw it, was about to explode into a fight full of words magnified by uncompromising feeling.

"I'm piss-sick of this," I directed at Leon, who ignored my childish outburst. This fuelled the fire. I loathed his, as it appeared, smug silence.

"Can you read a fucking map or what? We've already canoed about two days' worth of your dipstick mistakes."

"Oh please don't act like such a wet fart," he retorted.

"If this fucking centre isn't around the next estuary, I'm pulling up. I've had enough!" I yelled back.

"I've got the tent and cooker, so fuck you," came the reply.

"I'm piss sick of your lazy-arsed approach to this expedition, your shit company and fucking uselessness with a bastard map!" I again yelled.

"If you're so fucking special, have the fucking map!" Leon threw the heavy, sodden, laminated map at me. It hit me directly in the face. With this blow, thoughts of rationality burst into my head. Why were we arguing?

"Leon, let's pull in for a choccy break and five minutes' rest," I said.

"Yeah, good one," Leon replied.

Our tantrum was over, the air cleared, and we relaxed back into our usual compromising selves as I shared out the last of the chocolate. Killary could only be half a mile away. We had to get there.

Stephen Hanon, an old friend, welcomed us leading the way to the showers. He, as a sea canoeist, knew the value of this luxury on such an expedition. Piping hot food was on the table as we entered the dining room feeling refreshed.

Steve decided a pint was in order and so drove us the 16 miles to his local, over bog, rock and track in his red four-wheeler which resembled a small fire engine. To start her up, Steve had to handcrank it at the front, while Leon and I pushed from the rear. Once going, we all had to jump on whilst on the move.

The pub was also a grocery shop and post office, and all were still open at 11.30 p.m. On entry, I was hit by a slate-grey smoky wall, the rich aroma of burning turf and pipe tobacco. To my left was the meat counter. Two middle-aged, red-faced men, their pints set down, were sitting on either side of a carcass of ham with a meat cleaver wedged halfway in it. Further along a small boy and his sister (neither of them older than eleven) were buying bread and milk from the plump red-haired lady. She was serving beer at the same time. The long counter eventually led to beer taps, whisky and gin bottles, and the turf fire. By the fire, set on bare earth with no grate, sat an old grey-haired disfigured man. He was unshaven, his hair in clumps and his jacket, still on, was held around his thin frame by a cord.

Wednesday 3rd August
Little Killary to Achill Island. Distance: 20 miles.

After saying out goodbyes at Little Killary Adventure Centre, we headed off at high tide at 3.15 p.m., arriving on Clear Island at 6.30ish. It was a flat, calm sea with a warm sun promoting the beautiful mountains and green fields of Connemara. As we arrived at the harbour, so too did the beer delivery for the only pub on this island. It came from the mainland by a boat, filled to the brim, and was collected from the small harbour by a fleet of tractors. It also had on board groceries, people and other items only available from the mainland. With the tractors, 20 or 30 people crammed onto the tiny harbour, collecting their parcels, creating an excited atmosphere of toing and froing.

We changed and headed to the nearest pub – first, to cash a cheque, as neither of us had a penny, and secondly to get a feed of potatoes. We managed both and left Clare Island heading toward Achill at about 8.30 p.m., just as the sun was setting over a rainbow. It was an idyllic start to an evening into night paddle. The Achill Island lighthouse in the distance could just be seen, guiding us across.

Entering Achill Sound (the water running between Achill Island and the mainland) our destination lay four miles up the Sound, at the bridge between the two. It became obvious quite soon that the Sound was not running in our favour. This made it rather harder paddling than we'd have liked, but we carried on into the darkness of nightfall. The tide was going out, so we feared the Sound might dry up like an estuary. This looked imminent when half a mile from our decided destination, we hit a sandbank. It was now blacker than a black thing. All we could see were car lights on the Achill bridge and the odd light from a house: my watch beeped out the eleventh hour. We really didn't want to get out of our boats in the middle of a sandbank, as quite often there are dangerous spots of sinking sand or mud that, especially in the dark, could cause problems to say the least. So instead, like two cumbersome seals out of water, we pushed and pulled with our hands, making very slow headway until, after what seemed an age, we found a beach leading to what might be land. Both of us were still in high spirits, laughing loudly as we made our way. If only we'd checked the drying heights on the nautical charts, none of this would be happening. But it wasn't a big deal - quite funny in fact. We navigated round Loop Head in a Force 4, and after a three-hour approach got the tides right for Blasket Sound. Now, by comparison, this was a laughable error to make.

We exited our boats, pulling and carrying them up over seaweed-covered rocks, slipping and falling like two drunks making their way home in pouring rain. Once out of the seaweed, we tried to work out the topography ahead of us. It appeared to be a turf bog - just what we didn't need! After about 40 minutes of looking about and marching around, we found nowhere dry to pitch our tent. We decided instead to leave on our wetsuits and kayaking gear and wait for the next tide, some six hours away. I curled up, half-in and half-out of my boat, covered partially by the tent and a dry bag. "No," said Leon, after about 15 minutes, "I've had enough of this, I'm finding a way to get to that house." The house in question was only 500 yards away - we'd even seen someone in the window earlier. I, on the other hand was almost asleep, quite content in my damp but warm nest. "Come on," Leon said.
"Oh, do we have to?" I pleaded. With that, Leon was up - so sleepily and reluctantly, I followed.

84

We started over a barbed wire fence, then fell into a boggy ditch. Next came a cowpat, then thistles and brambles. It was like an S.A.S. assault course - after another ditch and fence we'd made it to the back door of the house. With a light coming from a crack in the curtain, I could just make out the time on my watch: it was a quarter to one. I knocked on the door and waited - nothing. "Leon, your turn, give it a good one," I said.
"Okay."
There was a shuffling of feet, some voices and the door was opened.
"Well lads," said the voice, "You've picked the weather." It was still bucketing down.
"Sorry to bother you at this late hour," I said, "but we've..." I went on to explain our predicament.
"I'd offer you a bed, but sure, I have the daughter here with the grandchildren. Anyway put ye tent up in the field."
He put on his car headlights so we could make our way back down to the boats. A thoughtful gesture, but it made little difference to our assault course.

Within half an hour we were in our tent, snug as bugs, listening to the rain beating down. Both drifting into slumber, we stirred to hear hooves and heavy breathing through large nostrils. A very inquisitive cow was visiting our nest. The thing is with cows, they are very nosey. But worse, they are also clumsy and have been the bane of many a camper, wrecking tents, stoves and anything else, new to their investigative minds. This one was no exception, I've always been wary of cows and bulls ever since being chased by a mad grey bull. But Leon was the brave one where cows were concerned. He unzipped the tent and shouted some obscenities which seemed to do the trick.

I was just nodding off when Mrs Moo came back, this time escorting a friend, to check us out. Leon again did his stuff, but the cows didn't take a blind bit of notice - safety in numbers, I guess.

There was nothing else for it - we had to move, as they weren't about to. The only other spot was outside the house. So back over the assault course, this time carrying a dome tent full of kit, dressed in a pair of skimpy boxer shorts, rain still lashing down and the bloody cows following. About halfway up the field, Leon had had enough. He didn't say anything. All I saw was a piece of 4 by 4 fly over my head and hit the cow full on. "Oh shit," I said, "I wish you hadn't done that." The cow, now looking very pissed off, was making a beeline for us. "Run!" I shouted, "This cow thinks she's a bull!" Laughing, we only just made it to the fence, hurdled it, and landed face down in mud and straw. Luckily, the cow (or cows) were not interested in the tent, just in the two, very wet lads standing in their underwear.

To retrieve our tent, Leon had a plan. I was to distract the mad cow by running across the field, while he would get the tent and somehow carry it over the fence. The cow took the bait initially, then saw Leon and the tent and turned tail, hammering at him. Anyway, eventually after much running and decoying we made it, tent intact. At 3.00 a.m., we were curled up in our tent for the night, at last.

Thursday 4th August
Achill Island to Dooyork to Porturlin. Distance: 22 miles. Duration: 7 hours. Sea state: flat. Weather: north, north-westerly F1 - 2, sunny.

With rain hammering down on the tent, we stirred at about 8.00 a.m., very quickly deciding to roll over and sleep on. After a couple more attempts to rise, we eventually crawled into daylight at 12 noon. The tide comes in and out in cycles of six hours. Therefore, it was just as we'd left it last night, the Sound still dry, and it would be for at least another three hours. This suited us both as we fancied a look around Achill and a bite to eat. We arrived an hour and a half later at Sweeney's bar to be told breakfast was over, lunch would start in about an hour, but tea and toast would be served in between. So tea and toast it was, followed by lunch, followed by our old favourite: apple pie, ice cream and fresh cream. Hardly able to move, I slumped writing postcards and reading the numerous dailies littered about the table.

By 3.30 p.m., we were both at sea and heading north in a headwind on a pretty shitty dull day. Our spirits were rather high, laughing about the night before and feeling full of good food. We arrived at Dooyork on a pebble beach and made our way across boggy fields towards where we thought the road lay, in search of a pub and more food. Leon spotted a car and raised his thumb. Amazingly, it stopped. Leon jumped the fence. I was close behind, brushing my teeth as I ran. Still brushing, I jumped into the car and we were off. A rather pretty and intoxicated young lady was our chauffeur. She chatted and laughed as she dropped us off, saying she'd never been hailed from a field before, neither had anyone brushed their teeth in her mother's car. I feasted for the second time that day and was just settling down to watch a bit of television. It dawned on both of us, almost simultaneously, that we hadn't a clue where we'd left our boats and tent or indeed, where we were. It was pitch black outside and there were three roads leading from the pub.

The car that brought us was parked nearby – I decided to knock on the door and see what would happen. "Hi, we're back again. I'm afraid with the excitement of getting a lift, neither of us took any notice of where you picked us up and so we're a little lost," I said sheepishly.
"Who's that?" said a loud female Irish voice.
"Those two lads I lifted earlier."
With that, the voice appeared. It was the mother of the house.
"Come in lads, you're welcome. Sit down," she said ushering us into the warm kitchen. "Now, canoes is it? You're two brave fellas to go out in those seas that have claimed so many lives," she continued putting the tea on. "You'll take tea or would ye like a drop of whisky to warm ye up?"
"No, no tea would be fine."
After more chat, mainly from the mother, the daughter was told to go and make up the spare room and under no account were we to camp out tonight. We, of course, didn't argue and relaxed into more conversation and succumbed to a drop or two of whisky.

CHAPTER 6

DONEGAL, HALF-WAY AND THE GARDA ARE CALLED. STOLEN KAYAKS

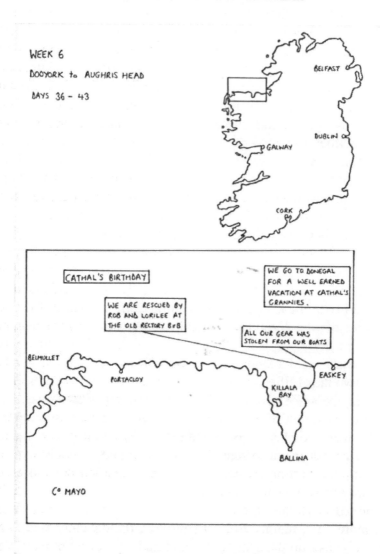

WEEK 6

DOOYORK to AUGHRIS HEAD

DAYS 36 - 43

BELFAST

GALWAY

DUBLIN

CORK

CATHAL'S BIRTHDAY

WE GO TO DONEGAL FOR A WELL EARNED VACATION AT CATHAL'S GRANNIES.

WE ARE RESCUED BY ROB AND LORILEE AT THE OLD RECTORY B&B

ALL OUR GEAR WAS STOLEN FROM OUR BOATS

BELMULLET

PORTACLOY

EASKEY

KILLALA BAY

BALLINA

Cº MAYO

Saturday 6th August
From Dous to Easkey Beach. Distance: 33 miles. Weather: mostly sunny, with hail and rain.

We started earlier than usual today. Our aim was to put in the mileage so we could take a much-needed two to three days' rest once we arrived in Donegal, which would hopefully be by Sunday. Although realistically, our sights may have been set a little high. Donegal was still a week away and we hadn't taken a full day's rest for some time. The only thing keeping us going was our dogged determination, knowing Donegal was slowly getting closer.

Cathy, our good friend from England, was once again flying over to see us. This would change our focus: we were both looking forward to someone else to talk to, rather than each other.

Unfortunately we'd had no breakfast and after three hours (or 10 miles) of paddling, Leon and I were ravenous. So we pulled in on a rock for a sandwich of stale bread, mouldy cheese and smelly sardines in tomato. After eating it, I wished I'd not bothered. It kept repeating itself like a bad dream. The taste kept coming back until, combined with the smell of bird droppings wafting from the high picturesque cliffs, it all became too much. Up it all came in one big retch. Feeling much better, I started to paddle and daydream about my favourite topic of the moment: finishing this trip at Rosslare. We landed at 4.30 p.m. on a tiny slipway; it was a second lunch and rehydration stop. The day was dry and warm. Unfortunately both our water supplies were exhausted. After walking for around a mile, we managed to pick up a lift from a lady with pink nails, pink eye shadow, and pink lipstick all pulled together by a pink dress. We squashed into the car with her mother-in-law, father and four children all chattering and asking us questions about the two canoes they'd seen. We were dropped at the only pub in town and, to the owner's surprise, we ordered six bowls of ice cream and fruit cocktail and ate the lot. We were in need of a big sugar hit.

The weather had changed. A slight headwind was blowing

against us, the tide was flowing with us, and this combination acted to piss us both off as saltwater continually battered our faces and eyes. We were now level with Easkey beach, after a two-mile open crossing. Leon was not his usual mild-mannered self, instead pissed off mainly due to cocking up the crossing. He'd led all the way, but had not picked the right line. This had meant gaining less mileage, taking more time. The wind, still against us, was becoming much stronger. I expressed concern but Leon ignored it, wanting to round a rather tricky headland before calling it a day. His decision to continue seemed foolish and irrational.

"Leon!" I shouted trying to be heard over the wind. "This is a waste of time, we're both knackered."
"No, we're going round. Just keep at it," his reply. Easkey is known all over Great Britain for its large volume surf. This was now evident in front, where huge surf was rolling in.
"Leon, let's head in," I tried again.
"Just fucking keep paddling. I'm not stopping. I'm sick of fucking stopping," he shouted back.
I knew it was inevitable that we'd have to pull in; we were getting slower and the wind was still on the increase. So I shut up and waited for the inevitable. Before this happened, my attention was drawn to the beach where I could just make out two figures waving and flashing their headlights.
"Can you see that, Leon?" I shouted.
"Yeah, what is it?" he shouted back.
"I don't know - could it be a danger warning or something?" I said.
"Oh shit, do you think we've missed something on the charts?" His tone and face changed from aggression to a definite worried expression. "Let's paddle towards them, slowly. Who knows what's ahead."

The colour of the water beneath our boats changed to a rich browny colour; it was swamped with long swirly seaweed. I wondered what might happen if one of us capsized in this, but put the thought to the back of my mind, before my imagination latched onto it. The lights were still flashing and we were still unsure of what was going on.

Slowly, we edged closer and closer. The two silhouettes turned into figures, then people. It was Cathy! How the hell had she tracked us down? With her was a tall, casually-dressed man smoking a roll-up. We greeted Cathy with warm affection. She had become our morale booster and contact with the real world on this journey.

The sunset was an amazing jumble of blending colours. Not just orange and yellow projecting like a huge furnace, but deep blues, mad purples and greens. The sky had a dark black background and sea as a backdrop. I stood watching Leon carry his boat in this spectacular setting.
It turned out that Cathy had been concerned, listening to weather bulletins and thought we might be delayed. She expressed this concern at The Old Rectory, a bed and breakfast she had chosen to stay in. The couple running it took her to Easkey Beach to seek out the canoeists, and by a massive fluke we were there, barely visible because of the dramatic sunset. Both Rob and Lorely were English, having escaped London and moved to remote Easkey.

Leon and I sat down in the back of Rob's camper.
"Cal, I'm feeling damn tired. Do you think we should have a rest?" Leon asked.
"I'd prefer to push on and not have to come back on ourselves. But," I continued, "I do need a rest and not just a day either."
"Shall we take a three-day vacation, now we're over half the way round?"
"Yeah, the weather is going to be shitty now anyhow!"

That was it. We were on holiday for three whole days!

Sunday 7th August - Tuesday 9th August
Vacation - Donegal.

Wednesday 10th August

After our welcome rest in Donegal, we headed back to our boats rather apprehensively. My mother and father, who were holidaying in Ireland, kindly drove us back along the windy roads to Easkey. They were looking forward to seeing us in action, after hearing the story so far. Neither of them had even seen a kayak before and were shocked to hear it carried our sleeping, eating, and all our other equipment on board. They were also amazed we'd made it this far. My mother was trying to persuade us to finish our expedition here and not go on. Her motives, like most mothers, were purely of the protective kind as she was rather afraid for us both being at sea. It was probably worse for her as she was not a swimmer and could not appreciate really the medium we were in. She was not alone on these two counts, as many of the Irish stories and songs were to do with lives lost at sea.

My stomach began to feel very hollow and tingly as we drove down the final track to where we'd left the boats. I was very definitely nervous. At times like this, I just wanted to get in and go - no fuss - just get on with it. The 'fight or flight' feeling.
"I'm sure we left them here," said Leon, both of us looking about the beach from the sanctuary of a warm car.
"Dad, can we go down that first turning? It must be there - sorry!" I said.
"How did you get this far, when you can't even find your canoes?" came Dad's jovial reply. "I hope you both paddle close to the shore," he finished, laughing. Dad always laughs at his own jokes, probably because nobody else does!

All that was at the end of our next turning was an old school and fields. "It must be that other lane we were just at," I said. "I'm sure that's the beach."
"Yeah, me too. But then, it was after a hard paddle. We were hardly coherent with direction," Leon said.

We drove up and down, up and down, for about an hour. My parents were understandably starting to lose patience and we were getting frustrated. The atmosphere was beginning to crack. "Over there... what's that? I am sure it's a canoe," Leon said pointing offshore.

"It's upside down - it's one of ours," I said.

The horror and realisation dawned in a split second. This was the beach where we'd left them, someone had tampered with them. "Shit, shit, shit!" I said climbing from the car, knowing I had to swim out and retrieve it. Both stripping to our boxers, we tiptoed over the shingle and sharp rock into the cold sea. Leon had a towline around his shoulder.

"Fuck, it's cold - Jesus!" he said, as his body became submerged. "Bastards! Even in the arse end of nowhere, some shit rips us off," I shouted. By the time we'd got it on tow and were back on land, my parents were standing by the car. They'd found the other one.

"It was down behind that ditch. I think it's got a hole in it though!" my mother said.

"Oh shit," Leon and I said in unison. The hole actually turned out to be one of the hatch openings, but of course my mother wasn't to know, so that was a huge relief. Leon's boat, on the other hand, did have a small half-inch leaky crack in the hull. However, worse than that, every single item of equipment was gone! Tent, sleeping bags, cooker, distress flares, clothing, maps, compass, charts, hatch covers, even a full tube of toothpaste!

We were gobsmacked! Never in a million years would we have thought this could happen in Ireland. Both determined to continue, we needed a salvage plan. My parents, very concerned at our predicament, suggested going back to Donegal. This was kind, but of little use. We needed to be near the boats. "Rob and Lorely," I said. "They're bound to know who to ask for help." Leon agreed, and within 10 minutes we were back at The Old Rectory where we had stayed when Cathy joined us. Here, we parted company with my parents. They were both disappointed not to see us paddle, but even more for our predicament. My mother was in tears as she waved us goodbye.

"Right, let's phone Joe and see if he can help," said Rob, picking up the telephone. Joe was sergeant of the local Garda (Irish police). His favourite job, we were told, was to guard Mrs Robinson, the Irish Premier, as she had a holiday house in Easkey. Luckily she wasn't in town, so we'd have the Garda's undivided attention.

Two Garda arrived in a small white and blue car with a blue light on top. One was dressed in uniform, looking very smart. He had a large belly, forearms the size of a loaf of bread, and grey hair surrounding a shiny, bald patch. The other had a casual shirt and trousers tucked into a pair of black wellies. Both asked the questions and both noted down our replies - their names were Cosgrave and Gallagher (a bit like Cagney and Lacey, though not quite the figures though). Our main concern, at this stage, was the distress flares. They were, after all, explosives, and in the wrong hands could be potentially life-threatening.

"Ah now, if they blow themselves up, it saves us both time and money tracking them... and another thing," Joe continued reading from the list we had given him, "what is the dragon, a pet is it?"

"No, no that's our tent. It's called a dragon!"

"Right lads, I think that's all we need for now. We'll meet you at six o'clock on the beach and take it from there," said Joe. We agreed and the crime-busting cops drove off. The rest of the day was spent phoning around our sponsors, who were all incredibly helpful, to arrange replacements.

I have to admit that this drama, to some extent, was welcome. I'd rather not have paddled another stroke if the truth be known, and was almost ready to throw in the towel! But somehow, however close to the edge you get, something makes you or gives you the mental strength to go on. Leon and I never discussed quitting, ever. This, I think, was a very positive uncensored pact. If we had disclosed our true thoughts and feelings on this matter, I believe it would have put us over the edge and we'd have quit on a number of occasions.

Easkey, being a small place and all that, the locals had all heard

94

about our misfortune. Some were so concerned and ashamed to think such a thing could happen in their town that they'd told the Garda they'd send up supplies and that we weren't to leave until they'd called. Nobody was quite sure what this meant, and so we all waited in mixed anticipation. It was not a very long wait.

First to enter was Mrs Durkin, dressed in a grey dress with a brown shawl over her head and shoulders. She gave us hand-knitted socks, knitted for her husband's birthday, but under the circumstances he would have to wait till she knitted him some others. Then came Mr Murphey, one of the pub owners, bringing a pipe and tobacco. Next came Mrs & Mrs Murrey, of the local dairy farm, who brought us half a dozen eggs and two pints of milk. Grandma Doggon brought an umbrella: "Some fella left this in the sitting room two years since. I have no need for it, but I'm sure it'll keep the sea off of ya," she said, handing it to me. The visitors came and went with things to help us on our way - a marvellous example of the extraordinary generosity of the Irish people. My favourite of all the gifts was a young schoolboy who brought his sister's Wendy house, without her knowledge, to replace our tent. This, was returned next day, but the thought was much appreciated.

We met at 6.00 p.m. English time, but around 7.30 p.m. Irish time. Our two ministers of law bantered and laughed, informing us they had found the culprits. Hopefully most, if not all, of our kit should be back in our charge by nightfall. This was great news: the culprits were apparently a couple of young kids, just as we'd thought. Later that evening, the Garda turned up with a car full of kit they'd recovered. It was not all there by any means, but enough to continue.

Thursday 11th August
Easkey Old Rectory, bed and breakfast. Stormbound. Sea state: choppy/rough. Weather: F5 - 6, north-easterly.

We were dragged, half-dreaming, from our bed, to be told one of the distress flares had been set off. Luckily they'd managed to inform the coastguard it was a false alarm, before he alerted a full-scale rescue. However the Garda's dilemma now revolved around a partially-detonated flare. They considered our knowledge superior to theirs, based on the idea we'd brought the explosives to Easkey so therefore we must know all about them. We were, in effect, the bomb disposal squad.

We raced to the scene in the panda car, blue light on - not flashing. ("It hasn't flashed since it went through the car wash in Sligo, two years since," Hugh explained.) Joe told us that kids had been dropping rocks on the flare in an attempt to set it off. We arrived at a field miles from anywhere. Hugh had been keeping guard and was pleased to see us.

They'd cordoned off the field where the flare lay with bailer cord. A danger sign had been written on the back of an old Guinness poster propped up against a beer crate. We were given torches, ear protectors and oilskins just in case it went off. We were trying not to burst into laughter at all this commotion over a smoke flare on a cow field in the middle of nowhere. We walked over to where it lay. Leon picked it up and walked back towards the car. "Is she safe?" shouted the sergeant.
"I think so," I replied.
"Jesus, where will we take it?" he shouted.
"Usually the coastguard or a local chemist can dispose of it," I replied. As the Coastguard was a long way, we opted for Mrs O'Leary, the local pharmacist.
"Oh Jesus, don't bring that bomb in here - you'll kill us all!" Mrs O'Leary screamed.
"It's a flare," I said, trying to reassure her. But too late - the door was shut with Mrs O'Leary taking cover inside.

It was 5.30 a.m. when we eventually returned to The Old Rectory. Leon had given the flare a sea burial off the harbour wall. At around 10.00 a.m., we crawled out of bed for the second time that day, ending up wishing we'd stayed in there. The wind was up to Force 6 from the north-westerly direction. We were stormbound again.

Rob took us to meet a rather eccentric old farmer called Shouting

96

Eddie. He was aptly nicknamed as he came within about an inch of your nose, and whatever he said he shouted at you, while copious flurries of saliva showered upon you. But this wasn't the only reason for his nickname. Shouting Eddie also had a dog. It was a cattle dog. As the cows were frightened of the dog, it made gathering for milking easier. But while we were there, Eddie went to gather the cattle and the dog lay relaxing in front of the fire. Even odder, we could hear a dog barking and Eddie shouting instructions to the animal. Being a little curious, I enquired as to where the other dog had come from. His wife replied: "Ah sure there's no other dog - that's Eddie pretending he's the dog. That fella there's scared stiff of the cattle." She pointed at the dog lying content in front of the fire.

On the way back to The Old Rectory, we bumped into Hugh Gallagher.
"Hello, hello, are yas well and fit for a bit of music and crack?" Hugh asked, clapping and rubbing his hands together, like a second-hand car salesman. "My sons and a local lad will be over shortly, with their bit-o-crack."
I mirrored his hand-clapping ritual.
"Music? Game on," I replied.
At 12.30 a.m., the quad arrived - fiddle, flute and guitar in their respective mitts - and there was singing, music and merriment into the early hours.

Friday 12th August
Easkey to Aughris Head. Distance: 11 miles. Duration: 3-4 hours. Sea state: choppy. Weather: F3 - 4, north-easterly.

After six days off, it was like starting the expedition again. I just wanted to put some miles behind us. The weather was still foul and the seas rough with rolling surf. However, we decided we needed to get back in the saddle, even if we only made half a mile. It was more of a mental attitude, needing to regain the focus on canoeing.

Rob, Lorely and their son, little Phoo, waved us goodbye as we paddled off into the surf. It was a re-introduction by fire. My

heart was pounding and adrenalin was making my hands shake. The walls of surf were between three and nine feet high. I was, once again, finding it difficult to pull myself together, feeling nervous and frightened. It's amazing how you initially forget what paddling in these conditions feels like. After about 40 minutes, I'd composed myself and was again back into the swing. It was very technical kayaking, picking a route between the dangerous breakers, rocks and perilous headlands. Both of us were concentrating almost non-stop, so conversation was limited. It was only after a short chocolate break, that we started to talk for the first time in two hours, losing ourselves in conversation for not more than two to three minutes. But it was just long enough to be sucked into a trap. We were in between two huge breakers coming straight at us. "Look left, Leon!" I shouted.
"Jesus, face up to it!" he shouted back.
I was on its nearside, so I turned and paddled like stink towards it - this was the only way to break through, otherwise it would drag you and your boat into the rocks. I'd only put in three paddle strokes when it hit, breaking as it passed over me. I felt as if someone had punched me in the gut, leaving a winded, unpleasant feeling. I looked back for Leon and he too was clear - a sharp reminder that complacency was a drug to leave on shore. My deck space was looking barren as the breaker had swept the chart and chocolate bars from it, but still, a fair price!

We landed an hour later on a slipway in a small sheltered harbour deciding we had achieved our 10-mile goal for that day. It was around 6.30ish. Feeling pleased, we pitched the tent with the radio on, tuned to an Irish radio station. The sun was beaming and skies were clear blue. Hopefully tomorrow would bring a much-needed calm sea and south-easterly breeze to help us along. Time was getting short.

CHAPTER 7

TIME IS RUNNING OUT, DEAR HEAD MASTER.
NIGHTS ARE CLOSING IN AND IT'S COLD

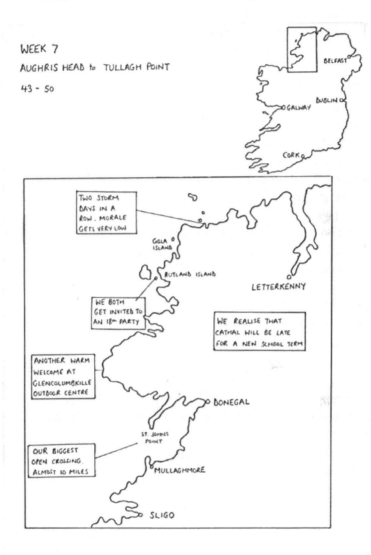

WEEK 7
AUGHRIS HEAD to TULLAGH POINT

43 - 50

BELFAST

GALWAY

DUBLIN

CORK

TWO STORM
DAYS IN A
ROW. MORALE
GETS VERY LOW

GOLA
ISLAND

RUTLAND ISLAND

LETTERKENNY

WE BOTH
GET INVITED TO
AN 18th PARTY

WE REALISE THAT
CATHAL WILL BE LATE
FOR A NEW SCHOOL TERM

ANOTHER WARM
WELCOME AT
GLENCOLUMBKILLE
OUTDOOR CENTRE

DONEGAL

ST. JOHNS
POINT

OUR BIGGEST
OPEN CROSSING.
ALMOST 10 MILES

MULLAGHMORE

SLIGO

Saturday 13th August - Cathal's 27th birthday

Aughris Head to Mullaghmore. Distance: 18 miles. Sea state: rough. Weather: north-westerly, F3, overcast with sunny spells.

I awoke at 9.30 a.m. to Phoo calling my name outside the tent. Lorely had made us sandwiches and a birthday cake to help us on our way. They had become our fan club!

I'm not big into birthdays, especially when you're paddling in shitty weather and rough seas. Mind you there was the occasional sun shining down on some of the best scenic beaches and picturesque backdrops we'd seen so far. The panoramic views were like something out of a John Wayne movie. The further north we got, the more barren the land and sparse the number of people.

Our days seemed to be getting shorter, with darkness falling at about 9.45 p.m. This affected us today as we had to pull in earlier than we would have liked, due to the fact that the next stage of our journey was a seven- to eight-mile open crossing to St John's Point, Donegal. If we'd continued today, it would have been dark when we arrived and it was a notoriously rough and jagged area of the coast.

The beach at Mullaghmore was enclosed by a huge breakwater; cars and people moved along its top. The beach was full of children and families splashing about in the water, playing frisbee and football, or picnicking, just like a picture postcard. The Irish must be a hardy lot; it most definitely wasn't warm. I felt a bit of a wimp in a wetsuit, hat, cagoule and fleece trousers.

The small village was tranquil, but yet had a holiday buzz about it. There was no shortage of places to eat: burger bars, pubs, cafes, and of course the beach hotel, with its sea view and green lawns leading to the beach. This was where we met its manageress and owner, Pauline - a buxom lady, full of spice.
"Ah, now I listened to you both on the radio last week," she said. We had been interviewed on a day-time radio programme. "Come and sit you down, we'll feed you up alright, and I

100

wouldn't want a penny for it. For it might be your last meal, God forbid. But with the rough waters you'll be in next on your journey, I wouldn't be surprised!" She bellowed this reassurance, without once taking a breath or pausing for punctuation. After the meal, to my surprise she walked in with a profiterole birthday cake, singing "Happy Birthday". Leon had told her it was my 27th - "such a young age to drown at sea," she'd said to him.

Walking down to the harbour wall after supper, I felt rather mixed feelings. I was quite chuffed to get a free beano, but unnerved by the giver's genuine concern for our safety. Was Donegal going to be that bad? Still pondering our fate, we sat looking out at the sun setting on the sea. "There was a terrible tragedy out on that beautiful bay," came a slow calm Irish voice from just behind me. I turned to acknowledge and enquire a little further, but was struck dumb. Two nuns, dressed in their black regalia, stood looking at me. Was this a conspiracy or some kind of omen - first Pauline, and now two sisters of mercy? I was still unable to speak. Leon came to my assistance.
"It wasn't two canoeists drowned at sea, was it?" Leon enquired, smiling.
"Oh, sure, far worse," said one.
"Not a bit of it," the other continued in perfect time, like an actress knowing her lines too well.
"Lord Mountbatten was killed out there with his grandson, while fishing", the first carried on as the other broke off.
"You wouldn't believe it to look at those waters..."

Anyway, the conversation then turned to lighter topics, and eventually we were invited to pitch our tent in the convent grounds and take breakfast with them in the morning at 7.30 a.m. sharp. We might have to give that a miss: 7.30 was a bit early for us.

Sunday 14th August
Mullaghmore to Glencolumbkille (Co. Donegal). Distance: 22 miles. Duration: 7 - 8 hours. Sea state: calm. Weather: south-westerly, F3 - 4.

Our boats had been locked up last night for safe keeping by an eccentric white-haired sailor. He wore blue wellies, blue trousers and a white polo neck jumper, all wrapped in a blue blazer with gold buttons. He was well-spoken with a soft Irish accent: "The years have since passed, when one could leave at one's leisure one's belongings, attended only by time and weather." He continued: "Sure, only two days since, I found a young and indeed pleasant fellow, attempting to steal a length of rope from my boat." He dashed about as he talked to us about the tidal streams we would encounter in Donegal, but he never once looked either of us in the eye. Just as I thought we were engrossed in conversation about the seas, he stopped in the middle of a sentence and was gone.

The wind had eventually backed to blow south-westerly, just as we'd expected, and indeed wanted. The seas were fairly calm and we made very good progress. The last two days or so, we'd both noticed the definite cold nip in the more northern air. Lunch stops were cut short, as we were finding we were getting cold very quickly. Our tent, which was recovered by the Garda, was now lacking a zip on one side preventing the door from closing. Luckily it hadn't rained yet, but it was a tad chilly.

Walking from tent to town, Leon and I stumbled on a small pottery shop. The potter and his wife, dressed in blue baggy 'his and hers' dungarees, offered us a cuppa which we gleefully accepted. The tea was of the herbal sort, orange and raspberry blossom, to be precise.

"Oh, can I have milk in mine?" I asked.

"You don't have milk in herbal tea," Leon directed, tutting.

"No, no, have it how you prefer," said Mrs Blue Dungarees, pouring milk into my cup. After more conversation it appeared they spent all day chilling, drinking herbal tea and making pots. A mellow existence I could get into, even the dungarees, but not the herbal tea.

Tonight, we found a tavern in the middle of nowhere. It was like going back 30 years in time. The floor was covered in stone flags leading to a glowing turf fire, with its welcoming and distinctive smell. The walls were yellow with many years' smoke stains and only one picture hanging on the wall: a nautical chart, showing the area around Donegal Bay. The locals called the owner Uncle Eamonn as he poured out the pints and chasers. The whole atmosphere created was one of a relaxed time trap. No one was rushing to do anything; there was just relaxed, idle chatter. It reminded me of the film "Brigadoon", about a village that comes to life for one day every 100 years.

Monday 15th August
Glencolumbkille. Stormbound. Sea state: rough. Weather: F6 - 7. Gale warning, easterly.

We should have known better when the Dragon tent was bending with the force of the gusting wind. But keen to persist as time was racing by, we launched at 10.15 a.m. into a gusting Force 6. It was blowing almost easterly - a very bizarre direction. In any case, it was offshore so potentially very dangerous, as we could be blown out to sea. This was noticeable as soon as we left shelter of the high cliffs. A team decision to land as soon as possible was made very quickly.
I shouted to Leon: "Let's land!"
He shouted back: "Bloody right."
We turned tail and headed directly into the strong wind. In front, and especially to my left where the rocky entrance to this bay was, I could see spectacular waves crashing onto rock and being forced high into the air like a firework display. We were far enough away to be in little danger from it, but were struggling for shore. Waves were picked up and thrown into our faces like buckets of water. After this, a gust of wind would pick up tiny, razor-like drops of water and fire those into our faces, leaving a sharp stinging feeling. We were only quarter of a mile offshore, but in the wind it took 45 minutes to get to land. Initially happy to be safe, our spirits lifted only to subside, as today no mileage would be made. At best we could make our way back to Uncle Eamonn's fireside and relax for the rest of the day.

It was as if we'd never left it. The pub, everyone and thing, was as it had been the night before - the same faces in the same seats. The only giveaway was that their facial stubble was slightly longer. Deja vu or what?

The locals were all very helpful and hospitable, and at 1.00 p.m., we gained forecasts for tomorrow's weather. It was south-westerly Force 5. "Ah sure, that's not too bad. You'll be right in dat," one of the locals exclaimed. He lifted his pint to his mouth which had only one tooth at the front. Everyone else muttered in agreement. His jersey and jacket lapels were stained and I could see why. As soon as his beer glass was back on the table, beer dribbled from his uneven closing mouth, adding to his soiled collection. We both smiled and said nothing, knowing a Force 5 to a canoeist was like a still day for a sailor, - useless. There were many positive things about a day off. One of course was rest; but the other, which may sound odd, was not having to limit how much fluid you drank because going for a pee was no problem on land. We took full advantage and drank much tea as we pondered our new and ever-changing travel plan.

I had had a slight pain in my right side for a couple of days now, and with one thing and another I hadn't investigated. However today in a coffee shop toilet, I pulled my t-shirt up only to find fresh and stale blood and a small wound. My appendix scar seemed to be opening, which was odd because I had it out 12 years ago. On closer examination, it looked as if something had been gnawing into me - a parasite I guess - not surprising when you think of some of the places we had camped. After speaking to the local parish doctor by phone, he was rather concerned that my scar was re-opening, due to all the abdominal muscle activity. He told me that on no account should I do any more paddling, or anything physically demanding, till he'd examined me tomorrow at 11.00 a.m. As you can imagine, this was quite a worrying thought - what else could happen?

Glencolumbkille is a popular tourist spot in Donegal. It has strong connections with the Catholic church, as with most of Ireland. However the link is more pronounced here. The parish priest had a vision to put Glencolumbkille on the map by setting up a small heritage and tourist centre. This he did over many years and his dream came true, employing many of the locals and bringing money to a much-needed area. He's now dead, but his picture hangs all over the small town as a lasting memory to his achievements.

It was a rainy drizzly day, with the odd rainbow. Leon and I wandered the town in and out of shops, wool mills, shops, wool mills and wool mills. Eventually, we came to the heritage centre, where a group of eight or ten small thatched houses had been preserved for Joe Public to experience days of old. The school building was on its original site. Inside were the original desks, and some children's school jotters lay open on them. You could feel the humming schoolroom atmosphere. From here, we moved into the village shop, where a Glencolumbkille wine tasting was in progress. Keen to learn, of course, we began training our palettes. I was told by one of the natives, who subsequently arranged a lift, that there was an outdoor pursuits centre nearby.

At 9.00 p.m., we heard the forecast for tomorrow: Force 3 to 4, north-westerly, rising to gale force by afternoon. What a pisser!

Tuesday 16th August
Glencolumbkille to Rutland Island. Distance: 22 miles. Duration: 7-8 hours. Weather north-westerly F4.

After a sound night's sleep, I crawled out of bed at the outdoor centre and had the novelty of a hot shower followed by a cup of coffee - rare and welcome pleasures.

The sun was shining and it was quite warm walking into the village, some three miles or so. The wind was still blowy and added to the combination of coast and sea, with hills of green, creating a romantic setting. If only time was on our side we would enjoy it even more, without the nagging feeling of wanting to continue.

The doctors' surgery was packed with old and young. On entering, the conversation halted and 12 pairs of eyes looked me up and down.
"Good morning," I addressed the waiting room. "Do I need to

sign in or register?"

"Not at all," came the sharp reply from a grey-haired man. "Just take your turn."

"It looks like a bit of a wait then," I said, trying to start a conversation to pass the time.

"You're lucky you aren't out in the street. It's quiet today!" the grey-haired man snarled back.

I decided to sit back, shut up, and write a few postcards. The surgery was very bland: no posters on the wall, no heating, just white chipped walls (with plaster only just clinging on) bordered by odd-looking people mostly sitting in rickety chairs of many shapes, colours and sizes. Two old men, each with sticks sat on my left: one walked with very bow legs, the other hunched forward, his cap set back on his head. The grey-haired man who I'd vaguely conversed with sat on my right, continually breathing and sighing in an exaggerated fashion, filling the whole room with his discontent. The rest of the room sat with hands on mouths or laps or sticks or even foreheads, as if waiting for someone or something to happen. No one spoke, just occasionally nodded at one another. After about an hour and a half I was ushered into Dr Heggety, a broad-spoken, stout man with grey hair and brown-rimmed glasses.

"Thanks for seeing me Doctor. It's probably nothing, but you never know," I said.

"Ah sure, we'd better be safe than sorry now," Dr Heggety replied, standing up. "Can you climb up onto the couch, drop your trousers and pull up your jumper?" He pointed to a bed covered in instruments and bottles of medicine. "That bed?" I said pointing.

"Aye, that's the one. Don't worry about all that, just brush it to one side or sit on it," he said, writing something down on a pad. Then up he jumped and walked towards me.

"Now then... no lumps, good... No ulceration, good... Any pain at all?" he asked while still prodding me.

"No, not really."

"Ya, ya, ya. I think you're okayish - not too serious anyway. Pull up your trousers." He walked back to his desk.

"I haven't got what you need for that parasite, but sure, I have an old tube of cream. It'll do you no harm," he said, handing me a white tube. "If it gets any worse I'd see a doctor at your next stop. Good luck to you and may God go wit ya." He finished shaking my hand and led me to the door. I think he was demonstrating a kind of inverted placebo effect, telling the patient the treatment was useless first. I left, content in the knowledge that it wasn't that bad. Indeed, I healed up soon after this visit!

I met up with Leon who had gained the latest weather forecast and consumed copious cups and pots of tea in Uncle Eamonn's pub. The forecast was not perfect, but good enough for us to paddle: Force 3 to 4 south-westerly, changing to Force 1 to 2 by evening. We were in our boats and on the water by 2.15 p.m. and had covered a distance of 22 miles by 9.45 p.m.

Around Dunlow at low tide, we were met by around 40 or 50 seals converging on rocks and basking in the water. It was good to see and watch them play, following our boats. The more you ignored them, the more inquisitive they became. The day's paddle had been filled with variety. Not just wildlife but scenery, weather and sea state: from blinding sun to fog and rain, from flat calm to raging surf and waves. As dusk fell, I noticed some people on Rutland Island and decided to ask where Burtonport was as it had to be close.
"Excuse me, could you tell me where Burtonport is please?" I shouted.
"Do'ye want a drink?" came the reply. "Come on up and get a drink."
"I'd love to," I shouted, pulling into the side and exiting the boat. Leon followed alongside.
"Come in, come in, you're welcome." Our host ushered us into his house and into the kitchen. "A beer lads - or wine? Or both?" he asked.
"Beer would be great," Leon said.
"Yep, make it two," I added.
It later transpired we were in Edmund's house and it was his son's 18th birthday. So they'd invited the neighbours over for a dinner party to celebrate. I say 'neighbours' but Rutland Island is, for the best part, unoccupied. However there are about six

houses on this small island that had been bought and restored, which were now used as holiday homes. This one was no exception. There were about 15 guests ranging from three years to 70 years old, all drinking and making merry. Both still in our wetsuits and canoeing gear, Leon and I were ushered to a table and seated. Out of nowhere came two plates of spuds, frankfurters, salad and mustard. They were plonked in front of us on the table and we heartily tucked in. "Have you boys not eaten for a week?" the lady of the house enquired as we devoured our grub: it must have been the wild man coming ashore or something. It was then pointed out to us: "By the Gods above, how did you make it this far in one bit, when you couldn't find Burtonport, sure it's opposite!" A grey-haired man in a sailor's cap, and slurring his slurs, pointed across the way.

The house had recently been renovated from a dilapidated pub. It had its own jetty leading up to the main, middle level: a conservatory which housed the kitchen and breakfast rooms. The living room had at its heart an open fire, and the whole room was decorated in pine with the odd rug on the floor and chart on the wall. The lower level (the wet area where all coats and wellies were kept) was connected to the upper level by a simple pine staircase. This was also where the bedrooms and showers were. After our supper Edmund insisted we stay the night, and who were we to refuse such an offer as we chatted and supped to the wee small hours.

Wednesday 17th August
Rutland Island to Inishbofin. Distance: 20 miles. Weather: North-westerly F3, dying out to F2.

Leon and I were on the water and paddling away from our host by 9.30 a.m.
"Sure, will ye not take a drop eh tea and rasher of bacon, before ye set off?" our host had enquired while we packed up our canoes.
"No, thanks but we won't," I said. We wanted to go now, for the predicted weather was not good. It was already bad enough, wind and rain in our faces. It was going to be a hard day, with

few rest stops.

Bloody Foreland, poetically named, was in our sights. It was obvious by its large white lighthouse. It looked from a distance a calm and naive headland: it didn't stick out nor was it perched on particularly high cliffs. In fact, it was only barely out of reach of the sea and a farmer was ploughing his field, mounted up on it, right to the foreland's edge. Getting closer though it deserved its name, for hidden beneath the water was a coral bed. This challenged the sea, causing it to bubble and throw waves into the air, producing overfalls and a fast tide. From this wild water I could see the farmer, working, stopping, fiddling and continuing. The sun had broken through and it warmed him as he toiled safely on his field. Barely 300 yards away from us, but in real terms as far away as the moon. He stopped and stood watching us in our boiling cauldron, even waving at one point. Never has the definition and danger between sea and land been so poignantly underlined as today at Bloody Foreland.

Gola Island, one of the small peripheral islands of Donegal, was our lunch stop. The sun was still beaming. Propped against an old stone wall, I fell into a calm slumber, warm sun on my face and body. Gola used to be inhabited only eight to 10 years ago, but as with many of these peripheral islands, the islanders could no longer support themselves and had moved onto the mainland. Their family homes were still used in the summer for day trips and holidays. It was a barren, silent, beautiful place, especially on a day like today.

The still calm air followed us from sea and onto land, at Inishbofin, where we camped for the night, looking out on a view fit for the Gods.

Thursday 18th August
Inishbofin.   Stormbound.   Sea state: large swell.   Weather: southerly F4 - 6, gusting.

The dead calm of the still night seemed to have changed when we awoke at around 9.30 a.m. I was sick of hearing about the incredible heatwave in England - let's have a bit over here! The wind changed direction every half-hour, in between pouring rain and sunny spells. It would be easy to be a weather forecaster in Ireland. Just go for: "Windy at times, with sunny spells and occasional scattered showers." You'd always be fairly close. The forecast suggested yet another change in wind direction - westerly five to six gusting. If this carried on, I might start building a house over here to fill the time on these copious Donegal storm days.

The only place open was the post office, so in we popped to mail postcards and chance a cup of tea.
"Good morning," I began. "You look more lovely every time I see you, if that's possible." I was addressing the mature postmistress we'd met the night before.
"Ah, ye little devil," she replied, smiling. "Are ye off today then to the island?" She was referring to Tory Island, a tourist spot eight miles off Donegal. "No, no," I said. "We're stormbound for the moment. But it's worth it to meet a damsel such as yourself."
"Are ye on holidays lads?" she enquired as the post office began to fill a little. It was only small, so four people would fill it. We told her about our intended journey and how it was progressing. "Oh you must be mad in the head - the dances you should be at, not wasting energy at sea!" she said laughing.
"A cup of tea, did you say?" I chanced.
"D'you want tea? I'll make tea!" And off she went, leaving everyone queuing at the counter.

Five minutes later she returned with a tray of bread and jam, two cream doughnuts and two mugs of tea. "Now lads, work away," she said putting the tray on the counter in front of us. We tucked in as she attended to her customers.

Next door to the post office was Dixon's bar where we sat relaxing after our doughnuts. Leon had just set the atmosphere by shoving a few coins into the jukebox. We were both indulging in chocolate-covered fig rolls (a new discovery) whilst reading the daily rags. Our silence was interrupted and then destroyed by

110

the pub drunk - every pub has one! 'Why us?' I wondered, as he pulled back on his cigarette and blew it into our faces. I don't know which was stronger - the rich tobacco or the alcoholic fumes which made up this dense fog. At first he gabbled and hovered over our table asking questions, never waiting for answers, then asking the same questions again. When an answer was given, he would repeat it, linger on the last word, saying it over a few times. Then he would sway a little, stagger, have another sip followed by a drag on the cigarette. He would pull his face up as if in pain, stare at us, and begin questioning again. Occasionally, he broke off into a babbled song or mixture of songs, all joined by drunken phrases. He sat down next to me saying: "You're welcome, you're welcome, oh you're welcome." Oh no! He was now as close to my face as a barber about to give me a wet shave. I didn't get a shave, but with saliva and spittle I was definitely wet. Next came the squeeze and nip of the knee, followed by gabble and high-pitched laughter. He looked at me for a reaction or reassurance - neither of which I knowingly gave, just a polite smile. This however seemed to be enough, for next came the arm around the shoulder. Leon was sitting back, rather amused at my new partner – or rather, by now, my old long-lost buddy. Luckily I was saved as the barman shouted over: "Willie, you're wanted in the main bar." Willie stood up, wobbled, and slowly staggered next door. No doubt to destroy someone else's tranquillity. We slid back into our peaceful silence of paper reading with occasional comment.

After checking up the video camera battery in the pub, I decided the camera wasn't working. Leon looked at it and drew the same conclusion. It had taken a beating over the previous seven weeks, but at least it was insured. I parcelled it up and sent it to a television crew in Dublin - maybe they could help.

The day drifted to evening and then to night. As a treat, we strolled to the other pub in the village and settled in front of the television with pints in hand. We were definitely in luck: no pub drunks and "The Godfather" was on the box. Soon engrossed in the underworld of scintillating gambling syndicates, bent politicians and cops, and numerous horse heads in beds, we both completely forgot our kayaking problems of wind and weather. After four pints, a record amount for this trip, we both merrily made our way down the hill, across the beach to the tent where we quickly fell flat out into deep slumber.

Friday 19th August
Stormbound. Sea state: swell and rough. Weather: gale force, southerly.

The forecast had come true - it was blowing an Irish hurricane. Worse, the sea was up full of white horses galloping. "Right, let's not get pissed at the weather. Let's be positive," I said, trying to be positive, but really feeling pissed off at the weather. "Yeah," Leon replied, "Let's find a coffee shop just for a change." Unluckily we missed the bus to the small town of Falcarragh, eight miles away, but luckily we hitched a lift from a lady who talked the whole journey about whales, their breeding habits, dietary intake and various other whale trivia. If we saw any, we promised to write and tell her as she was conducting a whale survey on behalf of Cork University.

It seemed almost inevitable that I would not be back in time for school, so I sat down in the first coffee shop and composed a concise letter to the Head Master, hoping he would understand and allow this absence. It was trickier than it sounded because, the old Head Man had just moved on to be Rector of Lincoln College, in Oxford and the new one, from New Zealand, I'd never met before. On top of that the letter had to go to the school secretary to be typed, before it could be sent!

5th September

Re: Circumnavigation of Ireland Expedition

Dear Head Master,

Before Dr Anderson moved to Oxford I discussed with him the expedition I am now on, namely circumnavigation of Ireland in a sea kayak. In the event of this expedition running into school time,

112

he gave his permission for a late return to Eton. PIM (Head of PE) is aware of the situation and has agreed to organise cover in my absence.

Unfortunately, during the expedition we have lost numerous days due to adverse weather conditions, mainly on the north-west coast of Ireland; but our main delays however, which neither of us foresaw, have been caused sadly by vandalism of our kayaks and the theft of most of the expedition equipment, including distress flares, tent, clothing and other essential items. Luckily local police recovered enough for us to continue, but time lost cannot be replaced.

I expect to be back in Eton on Thursday and will of course telephone you after receipt of this letter.

I hope this is acceptable to you, as to stop at this late stage after overcoming so many obstacles would be rather soul-destroying.

Yours sincerely,

Cathal McCosker

Myself and Leon have invented a new game to pass the time on storm days. We eat and eat and eat, trying to get as many bits of crockery on the table as possible. Each piece has a value: a mug is five, a plate is 15. If it's ketchup-stained, an extra three is given and so on. I could hardly stand up yesterday after four rounds of apple pies, chips and cream cakes. Even eating like this, we were still losing weight.

CHAPTER 8

MOUSTACHES, NORTHERN ISLAND, COMPLACENCY, ITCHY BOTTOMS AND RATHLIN SOUND

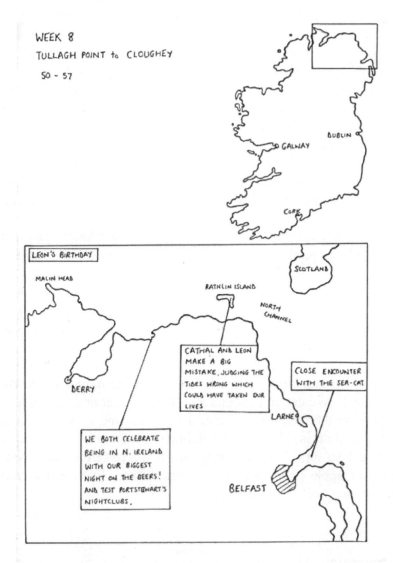

WEEK 8
TULLAGH POINT to CLOUGHEY
50 - 57

DUBLIN

GALWAY

CORK

LEON'S BIRTHDAY

SCOTLAND

MALIN HEAD

RATHLIN ISLAND

NORTH CHANNEL

CATHAL AND LEON MAKE A BIG MISTAKE, JUDGING THE TIDES WRONG WHICH COULD HAVE TAKEN OUR LIVES

CLOSE ENCOUNTER WITH THE SEA-CAT

DERRY

LARNE

WE BOTH CELEBRATE BEING IN N. IRELAND WITH OUR BIGGEST NIGHT ON THE BEERS! AND TEST PORTSTEWART'S NIGHTCLUBS.

BELFAST

Saturday 20th August

Inishbofin Bay to Dunaff Head. Distance: 26 miles. Duration: 7 - 8 hours. Sea state: swell with choppy sea. Weather: south-westerly, F3.

We made loads of progress to the base of Malin Head - the biggie. Malin Head was the furthest northern point in Ireland. It was a forbidding headland, notorious for harsh seas which have caused many shipwrecks. The day was warm and almost sunny, the paddle was one of the best: exciting at times, technical at times, and relaxing at others.

As promised, we were pushed along all day by a south-westerly breeze at our backs. This kind of assistance made a difference to distance travelled and one's frame of mind, boosting our morale. The seven or eight hours at sea passed quickly. Today, conversation flowed. We talked about the trip so far and wondered if we'd finish it. On days like today, singing was a good way to pass the pauses in conversation and lift our spirits.

On land and finished for the day, we met two holidaymakers on the quayside. As with many others we've met along the way, this was their special place: remote, peaceful and beautiful. They invited us to see their warm fire. Neither of them paused at the end of a sentence, continuing with the next. I have to concentrate and decipher, a bit like a French oral examination.

A passing tractor served as our transport to the pub. I hung off the back and Leon stood on the metal shelf, next to the driver. Any communication, other than the odd nod, was overpowered by the roar of its engine. By the time we reached the pub, I was glad to loosen my grip; already tired arms were now ready to fall off. Leon had a similar problem, his head bouncing off the cab roof with the ever bumpier potholes, and there were many of them.

Leaving the pub at 10.00 p.m. was meant to allow time to get back to our tent, and then early to bed at around 11.00ish. A battered old Peugeot pulled up just as we'd left the pub. A window rolled down and a beady-looking mustachioed old man poked his head out. I never usually trust people with moustaches. "Would you like a lift lads?" he shouted. We were settled in his car before he'd wound his window back up! I was thinking I'd be in the sack even sooner.

Our pilot at the wheel put the boot down and sped off. He talked at us as he drove but neither of us understood a word he said, but politely smiled and tried to explain where we were camping. It was obvious from the stench of whisky on his breath that he'd had a drop or two. This, I think, fuelled his incoherent babble and wild driving. He ignored us both, raising his voice and continuing with his coded chatter. As he took the wrong turning, I again tried to interrupt, explaining we didn't really want to go this way but still nothing penetrated. Eventually, a barely audible sentence was digested by our ears. "All roads go the same way now, lads," he said, looking at Leon.

"No, our road's not yours, I'm afraid," Leon said, smiling politely, not wishing to offend. This seemed to irritate our driver, as within seconds of this sentence the anchors were on and the Peugeot ground to a stop.

"This is as far as you're going," he blathered.

"Well that's very decent of you, taking us five miles out of our way. I suppose this is the scenic route?" I said sarcastically, not relishing the extra walk home.

"It's not my fault you fellas don't know where you are," he replied, sounding as if he had to walk the distance and not us. I climbed out and walked off. Next, came a string of obscenities from moustache-man and off he went - only for about 500 yards though, then we heard the car stop and turn around. 'Good news,' I thought to myself, 'he's obviously feeling guilty and is going to drop us back.' Not quite the right scenario! He drove straight at us, like a raging bull chasing a red rag. Both of us piled over the nearest fence, ripping trousers and skin on barbed wire. Now both covered with mud in a field of blackness, we saw him turn again. We laid low as he passed, then made a run for it, both of us oddly and perversely laughing and giggling as we went. Adventure was what we craved and now, like it or not, we'd found it. After about five minutes, the road was again clear.

So we chanced to walk along it - slowly making our way back, jumping the hedges, fences and ditches at any sign of a car's headlights. Eventually, we made it back by 1.00 a.m. and hit the hay, pleased to have avoided the mad moustache man.

Sunday 21st August
Leon's (and Princess Margaret's) birthday.
Dunaff Head to Dunagree Point. Distance: 26 miles. Duration: 8 hours. Sea state: flat. Weather: easterly F1.

Today was a big day. Not only was it Leon's birthday, but we would also round the most northerly tip of Ireland.

There were perfect conditions as we set off: calm seas, a slight breeze and the sun beaming. We could see Malin Head approaching as we came closer. It was an odd rock formation a bit like the Giant's Causeway: volcanic hexagon-shaped rock, set like a crazy paving ladder. The sea, even on this calm day, was bubbling white, cascading over sharp rock. The wildlife surrounding the Head was amazing. If you could compare it to Piccadilly Circus on a busy Saturday with all kinds of people in all kinds of dress darting about, only on a smaller scale. Malin Head was covered in shags, cormorants, guillemots, seagulls, puffins and many more; fighting, flying and diving. We sat and watched this moving tapestry whilst having a chocolate break and a drink. We were seeing something no one else could. It was a contented feeling.

Lunch was a sophisticated affair today. Finding a coffee shop near our landing site, Culdaff Bay, we sat eating breakfast, followed by lunch and a milkshake to celebrate rounding Malin Head and Leon's birthday. This must have been one of the longest lunch stops of the expedition, lasting nearly three hours.

Refuelled and in good spirits, we paddled off. We made good progress - finally pulling underneath a huge white lighthouse on Dunagree Point, only a mile across the River Foyle to Northern Ireland, something we were looking forward to. On the slipway, we were helped up by a father and son who were local fishermen.

Impressed with our craft, they asked to have a go, so we put them in and waded into the sea to launch our salty fishermen. They managed the affair quite well, but were keen to leave the canoeing to us. The sun still in the sky, we changed into warm kit, with beers in hand donated by our fishermen from their coolbox.

Tonight, we heard the pub before we saw it. Not odd for Ireland, a land of musicians and traditional music. This wasn't traditional though, but jazz, some of the best I've heard. The pub was in the middle of nowhere, yet packed out. I will remember the delicious prawn rolls.

Monday 22nd August
Dunagree to Portstewart. Distance: 8 miles. Duration: 3 hours. Sea state: choppy, no swell first time for a while. Weather: south-easterly F3 - 4, gusting 5 - 6 - blown off water.

As we crossed the River Foyle, entering Northern Ireland for the first time, the wind got up blowing across our path so headway could only just be made. On the beach in front of us, I could just see two green army Land Rovers racing up and down as if in pursuit of someone. They flashed their lights at us and I cordially waved back, thinking to myself how friendly they were. As we got closer, I noticed they'd stopped chasing around and were keeping level with our boats. Still flashing, the two soldiers seemed not to be waving but beckoning us in to shore. This puzzled both of us. Our only conclusion seemed to be that it was an army checkpoint. As I landed, an army officer approached. "Morning lads, do you realise where you are?" he said quite politely.
"I think so," I said, trying to sound in need of sympathy, just in case we'd done something we shouldn't have. "Northern Ireland isn't it?"
"Yes, but more importantly, you are in the middle of an army bomb test and firing zone. You're bloody lucky to be alive. We've been shooting at you for the last 20 minutes," he said.
Leon and I explained our journey.
"So you're heading north?" he continued.

"Yes, to Portstewart," I replied.

"Okay, keep going and I'll cease fire until you've passed by."

"Thank you," I said, and off we went.

I couldn't help but notice the refreshing and incredible change in scenery. From the bleak beauty of Donegal to the buses and amenities of Portstewart. It was indeed a welcome change to have all the amenities at our fingertips. It was noticeable that I was in the north, as it looked just like England, with distinctive red postboxes and telephone boxes, as well as familiar road markings.

We'd both been suffering with very itchy bottoms, covered in a red rash. This probably due to the lack of hygiene on this expedition combined with sand, seaweed and saltwater in our wetsuits. To prevent the problem escalating, as walking was becoming a painful chore, we decided to book into a bed and breakfast for a shower. I found the warm water painful on my arms and hands, probably because these were the areas continually exposed to wind and cold sea. I'd noticed that my hands had become rather rigid, and less supple than before; gripping small things, such as coins was markedly more tricky.

Next came a big feed, followed by a glass of wine. So far on this trip, alcohol had taken very much a back seat. But tonight marking Northern Ireland, and only one-third of the adventure left to go, a few bottles of red would be consumed in an orgy of celebration.

Tuesday 23rd August

Portstewart to Torr Head Bay. Distance: 27 miles. Duration: 8.25 hours. Sea state: flat as a kipper's dick. Weather: south-westerly F1 - 2. Occasional gusts.

It was not until 11.00 a.m. that we set off from Portstewart. We both had hazed hangover vision and a headache due to our over-indulgent red wine binge the night before. Our attention and thoughts soon turned to the vast beauty of the scenery before us. The Giant's Causeway, with its unusual shapes and images inset upon the towering walls of rock. With what had become our recent pinpoint accuracy, we pulled up on a fairly remote beach, which to our left housed a small wooden coffee shop. The wild men had become less evident - dwindling as the trip's mileage increased. From our boat we produced our finest picnic yet: chicken paste, tomatoes, salad cream, freshish bread and orange juice. This was all topped off with numerous coffees and cake in the coffee shop. We sat for at least an hour and a half, allowing our sore heads a little time to recover.

After asking two local fishermen at the start of Rathlin Sound, for advice on how to tackle this fast-running tidal stream, they left us feeling rather confident. Local knowledge of waters is always worth gaining if possible. Although it's up to you to interpret what is said and what is actually meant. I say this because quite often the fishermen we encountered did not really understand our craft and equated it to their own. This may have been a large trawler or small currach with outboard engine. Also, there is a definite language barrier, in that what is said is often misinterpreted - or worse, completely missed. The latter was our problem in Rathlin Sound. Something I found amazing was that many of these fishermen could not swim.

The tide was running in our favour, or so we thought, and the fishermen confirmed this. The fastest water was in the middle of the Sound, so this was where we headed: our big mistake, and a mistake that almost cost us our lives. At first, the tidal stream did as we expected and we moved with haste. I then felt something was wrong. We didn't seem to be moving forward, although at a mile offshore it can be difficult to tell at first. The way to make sure is to pinpoint a prominent object on the mainland, such as a house or large rock, then look at your watch and time yourself for four or five minutes, by which time you should have moved forward of this point. I did this and it appeared, if anything, we were moving backwards. To get a better idea of what was happening I did the same thing again, only this time I picked a point on Rathlin Island, opposite the mainland. Again it appeared we were moving backwards, or worse still sidewards. We were getting closer to Rathlin Island, yet paddling a definite line away from it.

This meant the tidal stream we were in was pulling us backwards and sideways. In other words, the flooding tide was taking us directly and quickly out to sea, and worse still, there was a moderate side wind helping. This tidal stream was stronger than our cruising paddling speed and, I thought, might even be stronger than our maximum speed of about four knots. I also knew the tide wasn't running at its fastest yet. It was increasing over the next hour. The harsh reality was that we might be swept out to sea, quite possibly to our deaths. A ferry glide across the tidal stream was the only option. Ferry gliding is a way of running diagonally with a tide to eventually cross it. We paddled like stink, with no let-up for over an hour, sweat dripping from our faces. My arms were in agony, but the worst thing was not knowing if we were moving or just paddling to exhaustion, only then to be washed out to sea.

After about three quarters of an hour, I knew we were moving towards land as I could smell cow manure in the air, something Leon had commented on earlier that day. Eventually, half a mile downstream, we made it to the mainland. I was shaking with sheer exhaustion accelerated by adrenalin pumping through my blood. We both looked at each other, knowing how lucky we were to be safe, a harsh reminder to us of the severity of this expedition. I honestly thought we'd gone over the edge, a mistake I'll never make again.

Going back to my point about gaining local knowledge: I went back to question the two fishermen. We had failed to interpret what was meant from what was said.

Wednesday 24th August
Stormbound and tired: Torr Head to Cushendun. Distance: 3-4 miles. Duration: 2 hours. Weather: F4 – 5, south-westerly. Sea state: choppy.

We were both tired and in need of an easy day at sea. Instead we received a choppy sea and Force 4 to 5 wind in our faces. After making little ground, we decided enough was enough and stormbound it would be.

On land we discovered the Cushendun Hotel, an unsophisticated and untouched haven where the owner was a well-known local character, if not hero. He owned and ran the hotel, was the district vet, had a law degree and was a Justice of the Peace. The hotel had welcoming large oak doors, leading to a wooden polished floor, in turn to a large airy room. This used to be the ballroom. We sat on two old, battered and comfy sofas, next to a large open turf fire. We ate and relaxed most of the day, writing the usual postcards, reading newspapers and dreaming of getting to Rosslare which now seemed imminent, we hoped.

I strolled out of the hotel, crossing an old stone bridge. I paused, watching a school of minnows darting about in the shadows cast by overhanging oak trees. The sun was warm on land. I continued past a post office and sat outside a Tudor-style courtyard, on a weathered brown bench, taking in the casual slow lifestyle of Cushendun. Very few cars interrupted this place. There were just odd-looking people moving in slow motion about their business. It was similar to waking up after a Sunday lie-in: a state of dozy, hazy stillness. Almost as if you've relieved yourself of your cumbersome body and are floating out looking in - and I don't mean magic mushrooms!

Thursday 25th August
Cushendun to Whitehead. Distance: 28 miles. Duration: 8 hours. Weather: westerly F1 - 2. Sea state: flat.

The sea and weather were pretty much perfect and we took full advantage, covering 28 miles and getting just outside Belfast. The wild men returned today eating all in sight without comment, conversation, or table manners. Lunch was chips, fish, mushrooms, beans, and half a loaf of bread, followed by cheesecake, cream and custard, washed down by pots of tea and coffee. Supper was a similar story: pizza, garlic bread, apple pie, cream and ice cream.

Leon was still suffering with a sore bottom, being very irritated by sand inside his wetsuit, and was now beginning to have quite serious pain, hardly able to walk on land. He had been having to stop off occasionally to rest. My urine was cloudy and nether regions itchy, a bout of thrush, I thought. At this stage in the expedition, our bodies had taken a beating and were more susceptible to these sort of minor uncomfortable ailments. It might be time for another shower and kit wash to lessen the effects.

The day's paddle was one full of flat seas, calm wind and healthy sunny skies. We covered 28 miles pulling into Whitehead just as darkness was falling. The nights were now drawing in. At the start of July it was light until 10.40 p.m. But darkness now fell by 9.00 p.m.

Whitehead was a squarely-built town, with nothing much to offer but smoke. The pub we found was very bland and not particularly hospitable. We decided that pitching a tent would not be the way to go. We knocked on the only bed and breakfast in town to be told by Mrs Rigby, the proprietor, that she didn't take guests at that time of night. "It's only 10.30 p.m.," I said to Leon, "hardly late for this country."

"Oh well, better pitch the tent then," Leon said, walking towards the boats. We'd only walked about 400 yards when Mrs Rigby called out: "Sorry boys, so sorry, I thought it was 2.00 a.m., and you were both mad drunk. You're the two canoeists off the radio aren't you?" she shouted down the street. We had, a few days before, been interviewed on another local radio show.

"Yeah, that's right," I said. "Is it okay to stay the night?"

"Yes, yes of course," she replied, waving us back to her house. Once inside, she showed us our room and, more importantly, the showers in which Leon spent over 40 minutes.

"Can I get you a cup of tea?" she asked.

"Oh, yes please!" we echoed.

She appeared 10 minutes later with a tray full of sandwiches, cake, biscuits and tea. We both looked at each other. After a huge feed only an hour before, neither of us could face this hospitality.

"Now boys," she began, "after a day at sea, I bet you'll polish this lot off."

"Oh thanks, what a treat. You really shouldn't have," I said.

"Not at all," she beamed and left the room.

"Quick Leon," I said. "Put some in your pocket."

"Pocket? I haven't any!" he replied.

"Well put 'em somewhere! We can't not eat," I said stuffing two beef butties and a slice of fruit cake into my trouser pockets.

Mrs Rigby entered once more. "Ah you've hardly touched it. Come on, don't be shy," she said, picking up the tray of sandwiches and offering them round.

"Thank you, they're very nice," said Leon with his most angelic smile.

Mrs Rigby again left us to eat, while she refilled the teapot. This time there was no stopping us. Sandwiches went in our underpants, out of the window, in plant pots and Leon even flushed a rockcake down the loo. It all sounds cruel, but we couldn't bear to tell Mrs Rigby we'd already eaten, especially with the feed she'd prepared. For the first time on this expedition, I weighed myself, on Mrs Rigby's scales (she assured me of their accuracy): I was 11st 10lbs. Before I'd left, I was 13st 3lbs - around a stone and a half weight loss. Leon, on the other hand, had increased from 9 to 9.5 stone.

Friday 26th August
Whitehead to Donaghadee. Distance: 20 miles. Duration: 5/6 hours. Sea state: calm. Weather: F4 - 5, south-westerly.

Today was one of the hardest days so far. I felt tired physically and mentally. The forecast was poor which bought me down another notch. Instead of a vertically straightforward crossing from Whitehead to Bangor, the Force 4 to 5, southerly-westerly wind meant we had to go to Carrickfergus, five miles up Belfast Lough, one of the shittiest and indiscriminately built-up areas in Northern Ireland. It smelled, the sea was rough, and wind was in our faces. The scenery was that of cranes, smoke and industrial piping. I hated every paddle stroke through this nasty industrial cesspit.

124

The whole thing made me feel aggressive, irritable and quite stressed. I wanted the day to end as soon as possible. Crossing the three-mile channel was hard work: it was like having to do something that really wasn't necessary, needing some kind of justification. Adrenalin did pump when the Seacat car ferry, with its eight foot wake passed 100 yards to our rear, luckily not at full pace so we didn't feel its full backwash. Once on the other side, I felt even more frustrated at having to paddle seven miles to get out of this shitty Lough. I think the day was tough because we hadn't had a day off for a while; even on stormbound days we'd ended up paddling hard for at least two to three hours. A day off would have been good. Tonight we made it to a pretty country village, something you'd expect to see in the Cotswolds. It was picturesque and the people were friendly. In fact our tent was pitched in a local's (George Ralston's) garden where we were lucky enough to be invited to take a shower. Later in a local pub, things started to get even better, when the local R.N.L.I. man bought us a pint.

We have gale warnings to look forward to tomorrow.

CHAPTER 9

BACK IN THE REPUBLIC. FEELING KNACKERED, JELLY FISH AND DIARRHOEA

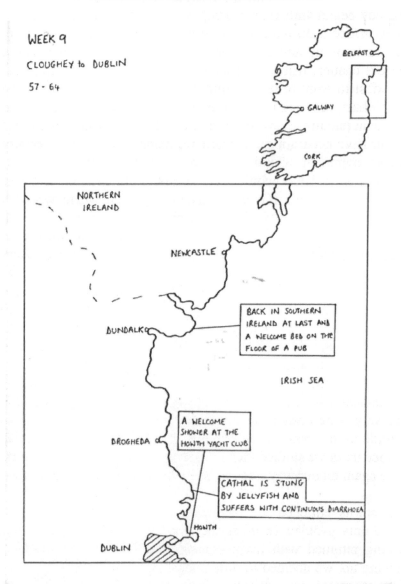

WEEK 9

CLOUGHEY to DUBLIN

57 - 64

BELFAST

GALWAY

CORK

NORTHERN IRELAND

NEWCASTLE

BACK IN SOUTHERN IRELAND AT LAST AND A WELCOME BED ON THE FLOOR OF A PUB

DUNDALK

IRISH SEA

A WELCOME SHOWER AT THE HOWTH YACHT CLUB

DROGHEDA

CATHAL IS STUNG BY JELLYFISH AND SUFFERS WITH CONTINUOUS DIARRHOEA

HOWTH

DUBLIN

Saturday 27th August
Donaghadee to Cloughey. Distance: 16 miles. Duration: 4-5 hours.
Sea state: slight chop, numerous overfalls. Weather: westerly 3 - 4.

The day began with George inviting us for breakfast. We rolled in at around 9.30 a.m. to a rather grand pine kitchen with the table set for us and the family. The atmosphere was one of relaxed chatter, while the mother of the house placed a cooked breakfast in front of us followed by toast and coffee. We could quite easily have sat there all day relaxing in this calm, friendly atmosphere. Just as we stood up to leave, Ma Ralston presented the wild men with a huge pile of sandwiches and cake for our lunch, saying: "I'm only doing this because I know how your mothers must feel, with their sons out at sea." We waved goodbye as the family stood on the rocks watching our tiny craft disappear.

Rounding a harbour wall just after lunch, Leon noticed we were being followed by a large adult grey seal. This continued for about 20 minutes: Mr Seal ducked and dived, swimming under our boats and keeping his distance. Quite soon there were 20, 30 even 40 black, grey and white seal heads bobbing around the boats. We slowed, sitting transfixed as they played. I've never seen a group of seals at such close quarters, as usually they stay quite a way off. Today they were within touching distance. I could clearly see their thick whiskered, wrinkled, wet faces, with two very large nostrils breathing out warm steamy air, as if from a kettle on the boil. Their heads were gleaming and wet. They studied us as we studied them. Soon they were gone and we were once again on our way, feeling oddly moved by this experience.

Our spirits enriched we landed near a roadside in Cloughey. We'd only paddled 16 miles, but with the combination of Leon feeling fatigued with his persistent sore bottom and the wind picking up, we decided to drop anchor. A definite change in the weather was here. A storm day looked highly probable and frankly we needed the rest. Concerned that our kayaks were next to a main road, I dared to enquire at a local house if we might pop them in their garden. "Of course, you can!" came the friendly reply from its occupants.

On finding the pub, I made a telephone call to England, to be given the good news that our friend Cathy was on her way to see us once again and would be there within the hour. Just what we needed to lift our weary spirits. On telling Leon the news, it was declared tomorrow would be a day off.

Sunday 28th August
Cloughey. Storm Day - the wind she did blow westerly: F6 - 7.

Both of us were feeling pretty shattered. The weather was such that we couldn't paddle anyhow, so there was no guilt at having a day of chilling and relaxing. Leon and I hopped into Cathy's hire car and headed towards Newcastle, over the Strangford Lough to Portaferry and onward.

Wherever we stopped or called in, there was a very definite underlying tension. The people we were encountering seemed continually on edge, not relaxed and chatty as in the Republic.

We all had a bit of a shock whilst driving along what appeared to be a peaceful country road.
Out of the ditches and surrounding foliage, six or seven police officers appeared. They were dressed in green body armour from head to toe. Around their necks hung the straps of automatic rifles which they clutched in two hands, with pistols attached at their hips, and walkie-talkies opposite.

Two in the middle waved us down whilst the others acted as their cover, kneeling in the road with guns cocked, continuously looking around. "What shall I do - stop or not?" Cathy asked nervously. "Looks a bit dodgy."
"I don't know. It could be a checkpoint, but how do we know?" Leon replied.
This show of weapons and manpower was something none of us had ever seen before. Feeling intimidated and uncertain, we could not think straight.
"We have to stop or they'll shoot," I said.

The car slowly came to a halt, and Cathy wound her window down.

"Where are you coming from Miss?" the policeman asked.

"Erm," Cathy said nervously, fumbling for the map. "Erm, I think..."

Leon butted in: "Newcastle, officer."

"And where are you heading?"

"Sightseeing," Leon answered again.

"And the nature of your business in Northern Ireland, sir?"

Cathy was shaking by this stage, quite overwhelmed by all this tension and questioning.

"Holidaymakers," Leon said - now leaning forward, giving the officer his full attention. "Why are...?"

He was interrupted.

"We moving?" said another policeman, holding his radio close to his mouth.

"Okay, move on!" And he waved us on.

Cathy drove off, still shaking. There was a very definite tension in the car, no-one saying anything. Cathy burst into tears.

"Come on, you're all right," Leon said, putting his hand comfortingly on her shoulder.

"Yeah, come on, dry the tears," I said, wiping her wet face with a probably very smelly wild man hanky. This outburst released all our tension.

At the next village we stopped, finding again no welcome in shops or pubs, and we headed back to Portaferry, It was one of the nicer spots, we decided, in Northern Ireland. Here, we spent the rest of the day relaxing by the quayside, watching the ferry toing and froing.

Monday 29th August
Cloughey to Minerstown. Distance: 18 miles. Duration: five hours. Weather: westerly wind F2 - 3 dropping to F1. Sea state: flat calm.

Cathy dropped us both back at our boats before she flew back to England, quite glad to leave Northern Ireland. The large picturesque beach we landed on yesterday at high tide was now just as picturesque, however, the sea was replaced by sand. It was low tide. We had to carry our boats over half a mile through sludge, and over slippery seaweed-covered rock, sapping considerable energy and time. Although it was an excuse to take an early lunchbreak before even paddling a stroke. We set off at midday, the sea and wind were quite favourable. Once on the water, little was said - both of us were beginning to feel quite drained now as the expedition was winding down to an end. I felt like an old man trudging along, winding my life down to an end.

There is, as I've mentioned before, a great deal of mental fatigue and strain involved in kayaking such a distance. Our bodies rely so heavily on our will to persist, having to force ourselves to keep going. I've often seen athletes collapse in a pile as they cross the finishing line of a race, the mental goal achieved so the body immediately gives up. On this expedition we were continually pushing our bodies to achieve our hourly, daily and more long-term goals. It was most definitely a joint effort between Leon and I. This acted as a bond, developing a symbiotic relationship - one was lost without the other and our strength was tied within each other. This was something I'd never experienced before, having to rely so heavily on someone else. I do not know if I could have undertaken this expedition on my own. But I knew as we edged even closer to Rosslare I would try to finish, even if for some reason Leon could not continue. I knew this would be incredibly difficult. One man attempted our expedition 18 months before us and aborted after five weeks.

It was late when we landed. A light drizzle had acted to keep us awake as we finished the last hour of the day. We were still saying very little, just the odd grunt or nod. We both fell into our routines of undressing and hanging wet clothes, dressing, pitching and finally rolling our boats onto their bellies signalling an end to this day's paddle. Once done, our minds turned to relaxing and dreaming, a state that always lifted our spirits, knowing we would have a few hours without the sea's company.

Tuesday 30th August

Minerstown to Whitestown. Duration: 7 hours. Distance: 23 miles. Weather: no wind, lots of sun. Sea state: flat, calm sea.

The combination of weary bodies, tired minds and the tension of Northern Ireland was having a very definite effect on this expedition. We were not enjoying the paddling or lunch stops as we once did. We had the kayaks' deckspace painted in the Irish tricolour, not realising the extreme responses it would evoke in Northern Ireland. With the continual talk of a peace agreement in Ireland, it seemed to bring everything to boiling point here. Today, this was marked by stones being hurled at us from a harbour wall; the boats' colourings seemed to be the only provocation for this attack. When we did land, immediately we upturned our boats one inward on the other, in an attempt to camouflage their colouring and our presence.

Leon and I landed quite late in the evening on a shabby beach in Minerstown. It was what appeared to be a remote spot on the map, with a meadow behind it. As we pitched our tent, dusk was falling and the air was still. Both shattered, we fell straight to sleep. We were rudely awakened at 1.00 a.m., by Mr Campsite manager. We had pitched unintentionally on a campsite - and of course had to pay £6! We'd been trying to avoid campsites, mainly because we didn't wish to be surrounded by lively holidaymakers making merry. Our idea of a good campsite was solitude, scenery and a quiet pub within walking distance. Also, why pay to camp in Ireland, when farmers generally didn't mind having the odd tent in their field?

In my sleepy and low mood, this invasion by someone I perceived as an ignorant and brash lad, evoked more than a nagging irritation. I was feeling bitter and aggressive, only just controlling my urge to pound his arrogant face in. Much more of this attitude I could not take; I was very near to boiling point. I've often likened a person's self-control to three containers: bucket, wine glass and thimble. Each one fills until finally the thimble, the easiest, is full. Then you explode like a tempest, unloading each vessel's contents all at once. I could not sleep for a while after this confrontation, going over the events in my mind time and again - feeling adrenalin fuelling my aggression.

The next day, with hindsight, he was probably just doing his job and pissed off to see us on his site. I'm glad my thimble had remained empty.

Wednesday 31st August
Winterhead, Co. Louth to Bettystown, Co. Meath. Distance: 19 miles. Duration: 5 hours. Weather: Wind Easterly F3 - 5. Sea state: choppy.

Today was the day we would cross over back into the Irish Republic. There was none of our usual apathy at getting out of our cosy, warm sleeping bags. We were up like a shot, packing kit furiously into our boat, keen to rid ourselves of the Northern Ireland tension.

Setting off at 8.00 a.m., possibly the earliest start we'd made, our moods were noticeably high, as was morale. We were soon heading across the River Foyle, dividing north from south. About two thirds of the way across stood a white majestic, proud-looking lighthouse. We sat in just behind it, gaining shelter from the strong tidal race we were facing. There was a tiny landing platform attached to the main body, a bit like a wart on a finger. A closer inspection revealed crude spray-paint graffiti - even out here this malignant parasite prowled, spoiling our proud figure.

Like opening the wardrobe door and finding that enchanting new world, we landed on Whitestown beach. Just as we hoped, and for most of the expedition had become accustomed to, we were met by an inquisitive native. Dragging our boats up to where the sea could not claim them, Leon spotted an aged man approaching on a bicycle. He came closer, stopping where we were now standing.
"Well now, you're welcome," he said leaning forward on the handlebars of his bike, like a priest about to preach from a pulpit.
"Have yee's been out fishing or what is it you're about?"
"We're just canoeing around, enjoying the fresh sea air," I

132

replied.

"And why not? I'd be doing the same if I was young and fit like you fellas," he added, his top lip flapping, due to a lack of teeth. I couldn't help noticing his very brown arms. They were large and overdeveloped. We both stood in our wet gear, in a light warm breeze, passing the time of day with Pete.

Once changed, we found Lily Flanagan's - "the only pub for 10 miles around" as we had been told earlier by Pete. It was a small and welcoming place with a warm atmosphere and an even warmer open fire balancing on an old grate. The floor was grey slate, all the walls were reddy-brown and the seats were numerous in size, shape and comfort.

The owner was very laid-back. Normally he didn't serve food. "Sure no-one ever asks for it, you'll have to do with what I've got," he said, and produced a tray. On it were chocolate biscuits and pickled onions on the same plate. Toast and jam with vegetable cuppa soup. The wild men ate the lot, almost eating the tray. We sat drinking stout, listening to a variety of music, pleased and relieved to be back in this atmosphere. Eventually after far too much Guinness, we were invited to stay on the floor as we were in no fit state to walk or even crawl to our boats or tent. The fire upstairs was still glowing as we fell into our alcoholic, peaceful sleep.

Leon needed to relieve himself in the middle of the night. After stepping and stumbling over me, he continued out of the room towards the toilet. After trying numerous doors in this darkened labyrinth without success, he headed to the bar downstairs where, from earlier attempts, he knew a convenience lay. At the bottom of the dark stairs, high-tech security stopped him momentarily; he then removed this plank of wood, which was preventing entry to the bar. As he stumbled further (not much further) the whole house lit up with lights flashing on and off, and a siren blasting out a high-pitched howl, that would wake the dead. Leon, obviously a little shaken, left the bar quite quickly and headed back to the sanctuary of his sleeping bag, kicking and stamping on me as he found it. No sooner was he in it than John, the landlord, could be heard cursing "that fecking alarm" then sleepily, and probably drunkenly, trying to switch it off which he eventually managed and he soon went back to his slumber. Leon still in need of relief, in fact in quite desperate need in view of all this excitement, once again crawled out of his sleeping bag and over me. This time, he was determined to succeed in his mission with the aid of a chair to stand on and an open window. He released his anxiety with comforting sighs and moans of relief.

On the water by 9.30 a.m., we had the wind and tide on our side, and taking full advantage we paddled 19 miles to Bettystown, just past Drogheda in Co. Meath. It is not something either of us would like to do regularly - five hours (or 19 miles non-stop) without breakfast or food en route. When we eventually stopped, I unfortunately stood on a large jellyfish. I've never been stung by one before and would prefer not to be again. But did count myself lucky as I was wearing sandals, so only half my foot was stung. The barman we later met told me he had been stung all over whilst accidentally swimming into a school of jellies, and had to spend four days in bed. As a result though, he had some cream which he readily gave me later that same evening. Even better luck than this, after entering Ireland's National Lottery throughout the trip, we had eventually won by having four out of six numbers. We got £20 - I know it's not the big £1,000,000 but it's better than nowt!

Thursday 1st September
Co. Dublin to Howth. Distance: 23 miles. Sea state: calm and choppy. Weather: easterly F1-2, sunny & overcast.

The tide was with us again today and we bombed along. Stopping at a small slipway for a pee, I accidently put my hand down onto a red jellyfish. You'd think I'd have learnt after yesterday's escapade! I couldn't see it hidden in all the seaweed and turbulent sand, and didn't realise either until the 15 to 20 second delayed reaction of the beast's sting hit me. Even worse, by this stage, I was standing in seawater, full of the thing's acidic poison, again only noticing 15 or so seconds after some had even sloshed into my cockpit. The pain was like a nettle sting, only about 10 times more potent initially, and then getting even stronger as time went on.

Within about 15 minutes of getting back into my boat, the pain all over my legs really began to steal my concentration and I was hardly able to think of anything else. I was trapped in my cockpit - unable to scratch, sooth or escape this poison. The feeling was of irritation, and extreme discomfort and pain. The pain was rather like a doctor's injection, just as the needle penetrates the skin. My legs then went into uncontrollable spasms, jerking and kicking. I could bear no more. I called Leon over; he'd been watching me and could see something was wrong. We were in choppy water, a slight offshore wind and tidal race. There was nowhere suitable to land: the coastline was covered with sharp rocks with sea breaking over them. The next place on the charts was a good two hours away.

"Leon, steady my boat. I've got to get into the water, this is fucking agony!" Leon held tight, as I balanced over the edge, putting one leg in at a time. As soon as I submerged my leg, I felt cool comfort. I knew it would only be temporary, for my cockpit was now covered in jellyfish stings. Leon was still holding my boat steady and I clambered back in. It began again: it was all too much.

"Ohh," I vomited. "Ohh," again. Then I seemed to pass out momentarily, for next I knew Leon was holding my boat, and my head out of the water.

"Cathal, Cathal, wake up! Come on, wake up!"

"What's wrong?" I muttered.

We were floating towards the breaking surf and rocks by this stage.

"I'm putting up a flare," Leon reached forward and pulled out a rocket distress signal.

"No, they won't be here quick enough to save us from the rocks," I said, feeling a little better after vomiting, but still dazed and in discomfort. "Put your towline on my boat and I'll try to paddle."

This was hell: scratching, jumping, and often crying out, as the pain lessened and intensified. At least, I didn't vomit again: I do so hate that feeling. After nearly two hours, we limped in onto a sand beach. Boys playing football stopped their game and came over to look. I don't really remember that bit. I was just lying on the sand, letting the water wash over, soothing my legs, floating in and out of consciousness. Leon, plastic bags for protection over his hands, washed my cockpit and wetsuit which were now covered with poison. I rubbed masses of the cream from yesterday into my legs, and after another two hours on land, it seemed to reduce the pain. Eventually I felt able to continue onward at 4.00 p.m., having missed the tide, although I had not felt well enough to eat.

The evening was sunny and warm: the flat sea was just perfect for the seven-mile paddle to Howth. By sharp contrast to this morning's epic, this turned out to be both a comfortable and dreamy voyage to the Howth Yacht club. We'd been invited by a friend of a friend whom we'd never met - Charles Blanford - to use the yacht club facilities. This meant the luxuries of a hot shower and we were able to wash our smelly kit. Yacht clubs are amazing places full of eccentric and passionate sailors, wearing old captain's cloth caps, and blue pullovers with round necks, shoulder lapels and patches on the sleeves. They talk and reminisce about races and voyages they've been a part of, drink large G & T's with ice and lemon, and refer to bar food as "galley tucker". They are like a tribe, having their own recognized chief and close followers. The tribe has its own language, dialogue and in-jokes, all helping to bond all of its members together. It's a self-enshrining mesh, all surrounded by the sea and her moods.

After meeting Charles, showering and relaxing, we pushed off to visit and stay overnight with Kate, my cousin, who lives in Dublin.

Friday 2nd September
Rest Day

At around midday we forced ourselves (neither of us feeling particularly in the mood to sightsee) to go into Dublin's city centre. Dublin has a lot to offer. It was the usual hustle and bustle of most cities, with unsavoury back streets and beggars. It also has some of the best street entertainment in Europe, ranging from a busker with a guitar to a juggling string quartet. It also

136

can boast some beautiful grassy areas such as Saint Stephen's Green, and interesting buildings such as the Guinness Brewery and Trinity College. I wasn't feeling at my best, in fact rather weak and shaky. Whilst sitting outside the library at Trinity, I began to feel even worse. You know when your mouth starts to salivate, and your body starts to convulse just before you throw up? I stood up and walked towards an office. Knocking and entering, I informed a very well-dressed and well-spoken lady, I was about to be sick and could she show me to a toilet. "Oh quick - that way!" she said, dragging me along by the arm in haste. "You're not doing it on my carpet. Do you know it took us four years to get a new one in this office? I'm not having a hung-over student violating it!"

"I'll try not to," I replied.

Once in the toilet she left me, saying: "Drinking was the root of all evil." Just in the nick of time: after that, came more diarrhoea and then vomiting. Feeling even weaker, with a throbbing headache, I made my way through a canteen full of students. By this stage I had double vision, was perspiring and was unable to walk straight. Holding on to chairs and tables, I bumbled my way outside, only to vomit again. Eventually, with Leon's help I made it back to Kate's, where I stayed face-down in bed, sipping water and occasionally vomiting.

I think by this stage in the expedition my body was tired, weak and worn. The combination of continued hot sun over the past couple of days, was causing some sunstroke. The reaction to being stung by jellyfish, and not eating yesterday or today had caused this exaggerated exhaustion. Leon too was on the verge of exhaustion, with continued diarrhoea and lethargy.

There was a positive side to all this. At least it happened while we were staying at my cousin's house, and I was in a warm bed rather than a sweaty, damp tent in a bog field. Also, Kate was a nurse which was always helpful in these kinds of situations.

CHAPTER 10

FLATULENCE. ROSSLARE

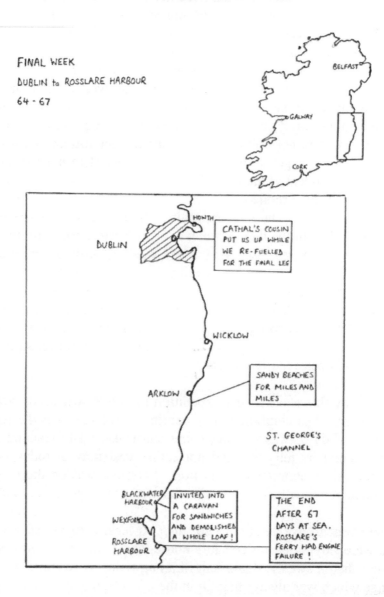

FINAL WEEK

DUBLIN to ROSSLARE HARBOUR

64 - 67

BELFAST

GALWAY

CORK

HOWTH

DUBLIN

CATHAL'S COUSIN
PUT US UP WHILE
WE RE-FUELLED
FOR THE FINAL LEG

WICKLOW

SANDY BEACHES
FOR MILES AND
MILES

ARKLOW

ST. GEORGE'S
CHANNEL

BLACKWATER
HARBOUR

INVITED INTO
A CARAVAN
FOR SANDWICHES
AND DEMOLISHED
A WHOLE LOAF !

WEXFORD

ROSSLARE
HARBOUR

THE END
AFTER 67
DAYS AT SEA.
ROSSLARE'S
FERRY HAD ENGINE
FAILURE !

Saturday 3rd September

The vomiting seemed to have subsided, but the diarrhoea was hell. It drained the energy from one's body, soiling clothing and underwear in an increasing attempt to soil one's dignity. The slightest movement seemed to spark a volcanic reaction of flatulence and liquid. My movements were limited to very slow walking or changing seating posture. When I was at primary school, a boy called Glyn had an incontinence problem which other boys soon discovered. After lunch each day if Glyn became overexcited, he'd uncontrollably pee and poo his pants. These boys would provoke an excited reaction. They'd make him laugh or cry until his pants were laden and a stench surrounded him. They would then chase him around the playground, a bit like 'kiss chase' only not so elegant, continually kicking him in the bottom. The winner was the first to expose his now mushy poo on the back tail of Glyn's white shirt. On such days, Glyn never made it to afternoon lessons.

Fortunately, I'm not being chased by those boys, but the outcome is similar. I know it's only four to five days paddle to the end. However at times like this, with a battered body coupled with illness, I wonder if I'll make it.

Leon visited the local video shop returning with five films. We sat, lay and sprawled, taking full advantage of Kate's warm house watching one after the other, pausing only to visit the loo which as you can imagine was quite frequent, or change the tape.

Neither of us, Leon nor I, would ever have imagined, under normal circumstances being able to sit for 10 hours just watching videos one after the other. This, I feel, was a measure of our extreme fatigue.

Sunday 4th September
Howth, Co. Dublin to Newcastle, Co. Wicklow. Distance: 26 miles. Weather: westerly, F3.

Trying to feel positive, yet still feeling weak and nauseous, I told

Leon I was fit to continue. Launching from Howth, the Dublin Bay crossing lay ahead. After the dangerous fiasco of almost being run down by the Seacat passenger ferry in Belfast Lough, I made damn sure of the Dublin Seacat's timetable, to avoid any repetition. Even with this taken care of, I was still nervous crossing the bay, looking left and right just in case and only glad once on the other side.

As we approached the mouth of the bay, I could see large container and passenger ferries in the distance. Heading out to sea, just on the corner of the bay it was noticeable that the water was changing. It stood out, a bit like a motorway on a flat landscape. This told us that overfall and confused water lay ahead. I was never quite sure how big or confused the water would be, but never took any chances. We both rafted together and I pulled on my buoyancy aid and warm hat, as well as making sure the deck space was clear of maps or kit. Often in this powerful water, kit was quite easily lost from the outside of the boats. Finally, I made sure my flares were at hand should anything go wrong.

If nothing else, this ritual increased awareness, adrenalin and hopefully a confident mental attitude. Once we were within 50 feet or so, we could see they were big - about 8 to 9 feet high - fast running overfalls. Often, canoeists sit and play in the rollercoaster of water for hours. Not us. We didn't have the energy for playtime, - we just wanted to get through in one piece and put more miles on the clock. This we did. Hugging the rocky shore for as long as we could, we then paddled ferociously like little frightened beavers.

The direction of the tide was very important on this east coast, making a big difference to how far or how easy a day's paddle could be. If mistimed it's like trying to run up an escalator that's going down. We get between 1 to 4 knot assistance depending on the area and time of flood. This can double our speed considering our kayaks go at, say, 3 to 4 knots on average.

The high tide changes every day moving forward by an hour. Of course, eventually, this means getting on the water at ridiculous times, like midnight or five o'clock in the morning. Frankly, Leon and I are not that keen about early mornings, so instead will battle with the tides as best we can.

Monday 5th September
Newcastle, Co. Wicklow to Clogey, Co. Wicklow. Distance: 19 miles. Weather: south-westerly, F3 - 5.

Leon had wrapped our small red radio in a crisp packet to repel water, and had firmly attached it with string to his front deck, giving us music and chat shows for the first time at sea. This gave us both a boost, being able to indulge ourselves in music and scenery. A welcome break from, by now, our repetitive conversation and mind games. The musical journey lasted for nearly four hours, until the crisp packet gave up whilst landing in surf for a pee, and our red radio drowned. It was probably for the best, as I could feel myself becoming a Terry Wogan addict.

I was still having some gut problems manifesting themselves in slight diarrhoea, but extreme and very smelly flatulence. In fact, the flatulence was almost uncontrollable. This, coupled with our daily mileage and wild man diet, was taking its toll. I was not feeling 100%. The last hour or so today was a real bitch of a paddle. The south-westerly wind began to gust at Force 5, and with the tide running against wind, it created much spray and breaking water in our faces. We landed soon after on Clogey beach feeling totally exhausted and I, farting like a trooper, on more than one occasion almost following through.

It was a very quiet spot, apart from my exploding bottom, we'd found. It's very noticeable how the landscape of the south-east is very similar to that of England and Wales with its oak woodland and privet hedges. Gone now were the stone walls so prominent in the bleaker regions of Ireland. It was, however, obvious one was in Ireland from the now notorious (in any eyes anyway) green and pink painted cottages and the very distinct smell of turf-burning fires in the air. We walked townwards, discussing what we would be doing this time next week - probably far away from this nomadic existence, donning the gowns of normality and rejoining the stresses and strains of everyday life. It felt like a very odd topic of conversation, as I don't think either of us believed it would actually end. After all, it seemed like we'd been doing it forever.

All at once, the conversation changed, on entering a small ugly motel. I say ugly, because in its perfect green and lush surroundings, this pre-fabricated row of boxes had paint peeling from sills, flat black roofs, and what appeared to be a complete lack of care in its image. This motel was the wart on Cinderella's nose.

After much polite debate and persuasion in the motel, we were told no food was being served and nor would it be until next year's tourist season - a long wait.

Walking back to our boats, with the prospect of no supper and putting up the tent in a dark car park, our moods were lowered. Then along our road came our saving grace: the Nolan family and their smelly dog. Thank God for that dog!

We raised our thumbs out simultaneously as the car went by, and it stopped a few hundred yards in front. We chased it and hopped in to be greeted by Ma Nolan, her daughter and their French visitor. Ma apologized for not pulling over at once, but went on to explain she could never find the brake as her legs were too short. As she drove to the nearest town, they quizzed us on our reasons for being in Ireland. The car journey was about 20 miles and I was beginning to feel quite uncomfortable as my guts were trying to expel an ever-increasing volume of very smelly gas, which I was trying to keep to myself. At last we stopped. As Leon was taking directions to the best and cheapest places to eat in town, I quickly hopped out and darted into a shadowed corner where I relieved my pain by equating gas pressure in my bowel with that of the evening air, in possibly one of the most sustained lengthy farts I've ever had cause to do. It was as long as it was smelly. If anyone would have had cause to bear a naked flame, I fear what might have ensued.

Leon wandered over towards me, only to be prevented from coming too close by the wall of pong.

"Jesus Christ, what have you eaten?" he said, "That smells worse than Belfast Lough."

"I know, I almost let it go over that last bump in the car," I replied.

As we walked to the recommended eating spot, Leon told me the girls would meet up with us later and we'd been offered a lift home, which of course was welcome news. I didn't fancy reliving a night rolled up in a hedge with a binbag for a blanket. In the hotel there was an obvious void surrounding our table, where no-one dared to sit, even though the place was packed. Maybe I could market it as an alternative to tear gas - for crowd control. As the gas built up I'd headed to the loo, closed the door, and relieved the pressure. This minimized the pong to some degree before returning to our table. It was, however, a very definite salvage job.

The two girls came in and sat beside us: one commented on a funny smell, but we both chose to ignore it and tried to play it down. Luckily - and I say this probably for the first and only time -they both lit up French cigarettes. I don't like smoking, but this did cover up the smell and allowed me to let rip at will, lessening my visits to the loo, and generally making it a more relaxed occasion.

After much welcome chatter and hilarity in pleasant company, we made a move to leave. As I stood up, the increased pressure on my gut was too much. The escaping gas made such a loud noise, I thought my cover was blown. But as I farted, a door slammed - so quickly, to escape the aftermath, I ushered the girls through the front door. "What a gentleman," one said, the other smiling and nodding in agreement. Looking behind me as I left, I saw the barmaid's face screw up as the debris cascaded all around. I'm sure she'd have had a few choice words about that display of gentlemanly conduct!

Again, surviving the journey back was difficult, although the opening and closing of windows made it a little easier for all concerned - that, and the effects of the consumed alcohol, deadening the senses.

"Where's your tent then?" Ma Nolan enquired, as we pulled into the car park.

"We haven't put it up yet," I replied.

"Well now, we've a spare bed if you'd like to stay for the night."

"We'd love to," I quickly responded, hoping the rooms were well ventilated, I didn't wish to smother in my own farts.

The Nolans lived in Dublin for most of the year, but always spent the summer in Clouga, in their self-designed, holiday home. It had large windows and conservatories all the way around, so ventilation wouldn't be a problem. The windows framed the surrounding green fields and sea in an idyllic and poetic scene.

I'd already visited the loo twice and didn't wish to blow my cover by going again. So I had no choice: as we sat drinking a cup of tea before bed, making polite conversation, I let a silent but deadly fart (they always are) drift into the room. It wasn't long before there was a reaction.

"You dirty bastard," shouted Pa Nolan. I looked up shamefully. He was on his feet and gave the dog a kick, expelling him from the room. Luck was on my side again. Lying in bed, I started wondering if my cover had really been blown and the Nolans were just being very polite?

Tuesday 6th September
Cloaga, Co. Wicklow to Blackwater, Co. Wexford. Duration: 7 hours. Distance: 22 miles. Sea state: choppy. Weather: south-westerly, F2 - 4, gusting.

It was bad enough putting on a cold, damp, wetsuit but today mine stank. This insipid smell was of body and bottom odour, as well as rotting seaweed, all enriched by the stagnation of seawater. We have on occasions washed them, but not for some time had this blessing been possible. However, there was no escaping, so gritting my teeth I pulled it on. Almost at once, the itching and scratching began - something we'd both become

144

accustomed to now. Just another part of the wild man.

Setting off into the wind, both our bottoms were feeling a little tender. It was a shivery feeling having water on the boat's seat, squelching around your bottom and legs, with the rolling action of your blade as we moved along. With time, the feeling of mild irritation turned to pain, resulting, in turn, to definite aggressive paddling. I was wanting the day to end quickly and so we could return to dry land and relative comfort. The wind dropped, but the heavens opened. The sea's appearance was completely masked by this pouring rain. Every wave seemed to be rolling in slow motion, like something out of a science fiction movie. The rain bounced off the sea's surface creating an elevated covering of haze, with light wind adding to the effect. Next came the loud drumming of thunder, followed by the sky's illumination by blue and green lightning, spreading across the whole screen of hazy grey. We did stop for a while to let the lightning pass over, not wishing to be its victims. We stood quite alone shivering on a deserted beach, watching the crazed sky. Eventually after seven hours, two pee stops and very sore bottoms we surfaced into Blackwater - just avoiding large rocks, a fisherman's line and dumping surf.

Whilst changing, we both talked of how this would be our last night in Ireland in a tent. Our last walk to explore and find food, our last... It continued... By good fortune, the fisherman we'd nearly collided with on our earlier landing invited us to his mobile home for tea. This too, again probably for the last time. Our nomadic existence was nearing the end. I was ready to finish but sad that with it. My freedom would once again be capped by the normality of everyday life and its values, or indeed lack of them.

I made a couple of phone calls: one to my mother, and one to Eton to let them know I should be back on time for the start of term. It seemed very odd planning so far ahead, as I'd become accustomed to living hour-to-hour or day-to-day on the expedition.

Wednesday 7th September
OUR FINAL DAY AT SEA.
Sea state: choppy.   Weather: south-westerly, F2 - 4, gusts.
Rosslare.

We moved off into light surf a little more nervous than usual, both rather tired and still not quite fully awake. It was not just any day. It was only 12 more miles to our original starting point in Rosslare: we could both see it in the distance. Neither spoke at first, perhaps in disbelief of what we would finally achieve this day. It was not as we would prefer, sunny and bright. Instead, the wind was in our faces, the skies dull and overcast, and the sea was far from calm. Not that any of this mattered as we both had our sights firmly set. It was a shitty and bumpy crossing over the estuary. On other days, we may have chosen to decline sitting out the weather in a cafe or pub. But not on this day. About halfway across, we did spy a family of seals resting on a large rock, a reminder of how lucky our floating vantage point was at sea.

Eventually we were back in Rosslare harbour, paddling towards the large ramp which had been kindly lowered for us, when we set off. After a final photo was taken, I climbed out and awaited the lowering of the ramp. It was the same man who 10 weeks beforehand lowered it.
"Well, fellas, you've made it - be Jesus, some journey!" he said shaking our hands. We pulled up our boats. "God must have been watching over ye both."
I agreed with his sentiments. But it was not man's God, but our God, the sea.

WE FINISHED! We were not euphoric, but we very definitely happy for it all to be over. We were almost in disbelief of our achievement. "No more soggy bottoms," Leon said.
"No more cold wetsuits to pull on in the morning," I added.
"No more paddling," he finished.

Ravenous with hunger, we headed towards the canteen, quickly realising our first priority was securing passage home on the

Seacat. When we were asked about luggage, Leon triumphantly declared: "Our boat is our luggage - all 14 foot of it."

"Oh," she said. "I really must ask the manageress." Off she popped, behind a large brown door.

"Oh God, not red tape I hope," Leon said. She returned with the manageress.

"And how big are they? How heavy? Where are they?..." she interrupted.

I told her the lot and eventually she gave the all-clear.

Full and content, we sat overlooking the sea. It was great looking out, not caring about whether the sea was white, or which way the wind blew. An announcement came over a loud speaker: "The Rosslare - Fishguard Seacat will have a delay, due to blah blah blah." We looked at each other and laughed. We'd finished. Nothing trivial could bother our warm mood.

I made three phone calls. The first was to my mother, who had followed this expedition from a mother's viewpoint. She'd had numerous sleepless nights and tense moments, when I had not been in contact for days on end. She was euphoric that we'd made it, but more important to her was that it was all over and her son safe. The second call was to Cathy who'd followed our expedition with such enthusiasm and interest that she had become a part of it. Her numerous visits to lift our spirits had been of such massive importance to us both that we owed her a great debt of loyalty and friendship. Thirdly, I called my grandmother because she was my fluffy shiny granmaw.

For this to finally have ended in relative calm, just as it began, seemed somehow not quite right. It was almost awkward or uncomfortable. Sitting looking out, I knew that I would not sit in a canoe at sea for some time. It was truly a very odd feeling. I would not miss it, but I knew I would return some day to once again taste that freedom one feels bobbing up and down out at sea.

TO BE BACK

Thursday 8th September

It was 3.00 a.m. when I pulled up outside the small, ivy-covered cottage which I hadn't seen (yet had dreamed of numerous times) for 10 weeks.

The five-hour car journey from Fishguard had passed remarkably quickly, after only moving at 20 miles a day in my kayak. The thrill of covering over 300 miles to get home made the drive enjoyable. Not to mention the comfy seat and dry warm interior - no wind or waves penetrating your clothing.

Fumbling to open the front door of Warre Stable Cottage, I realised that where I was aiming the key was not where the lock was. The lock, for some unknown reason, is set midway and not as you might expect three-quarters of the way up the door. The place was warm and cosy, just as it had been left. Feeling rather tired, and knowing tomorrow I would be teaching at 9.00 a.m. followed by various staff meetings and numerous errands, I was soon curled up and fast asleep.

Still feeling on a high at finishing one expedition and now starting another back to school, I awoke early to have a long soak, removing any evidence of the wild man. Unfortunately as I'd forgotten to turn on the hot water, it was a short cold dip. It felt very odd washing my hair with shampoo and donning aftershave. These two rituals underlined that the primitive expedition was truly over.

Colleagues at Eton seemed amazed that after finishing such a physically-exhausting experience, yesterday, I could be teaching the next day. I explained that teaching in a warm, controlled environment was a very easy alternative to canoeing in the wet and cold. I could enjoy a cuppa whenever I wanted, or sit and chat without worrying about wind or weather. The complete contrast of the two worlds made it quite easy - although a week off for rest and recreation would have been an ideal solution.

AFTERSHOCKS

Wednesday 21st September

It is odd at how simple pleasures, such as a hot cup of tea, clean clothes or even a hot soak in the bath, cannot be taken for granted any more. Their absence, or difficulty to obtain, on our expedition would leave a lasting footnote in my memory of their real importance in our sophisticated lifestyle of today.

In a similar light I was very grateful for the refuge and hospitality we received in pubs, cafes and Irish homes making the expedition easier to tolerate. However one of the most important things I'd missed was the freedom to relax in your own environment and not having to adapt to someone else's. My stereo was a great part of this freedom. I have not yet found another country where the warmth and friendliness of its people, their generosity and culture removes all the barriers that life so often puts in one's way. The Irish have a sense of living and enjoying life to its full - trivialities that so often blind us, seemed to give them increased clarity.

I still have not come to terms with our achievement at circumnavigating Ireland's land mass. Nor yet do I understand fully why we put our body, mind and spirit through this ordeal of unknowing fear and excitement - and perhaps I never will. I felt inexperienced when I set out and now feel properly experienced. It is two weeks since the expedition finished, and my body has not yet recovered fully. My hands feel tight and quite often I find them cramping, not able to grip: I guess due to the continual exposure to wind, rain and sea whilst holding a paddle. Both our lower backs are suffering pain, probably due to sitting for long periods in the boats. I have not attempted any vigorous sport as yet, still feeling rather fragile. My routine has changed and as a result my sleeping pattern will have to fall into line. It has not as yet, causing a few sleepless nights. All this, I'm sure, will pass in time.

Conflict on any expedition where two people are thrown together for the best part of 10 weeks is, you may think, inevitable and quite normal.   I can honestly say every decision made, was always a joint compromise between us both and quite often the elements. I could not have found a better partner or indeed friend for this expedition.   Leon's continued positive attitude, determination and support - especially when the chips were down or defeatism may have been setting in - was essential. It's fair to say that to get through, we both often pretended to be more positive and determined than either felt or indeed were. This too contributed to our success. I'm only glad that neither of us called the other's bluff!

I think we found the expedition harder than we had anticipated. The winds in particular, and the sea conditions that resulted, were very trying.   This turned what should have been fairly straightforward stretches into unpleasant slogs. However, that in no way detracted from the overall impact of the trip. Ireland is a marvellous island, offering a great deal in the way of beauty, solitude and commitment to the sea canoeist. To paddle around it was an experience I would not have missed. By the end of the expedition, we were becoming physically tired, and this was noticeable in different ways. It may well be that we did not organise ourselves well enough in terms of rest days. The rest days that we did take were often forced upon us by bad weather, and I'm not convinced of their value in terms of recuperation. I found it hard to relax, while wondering whether or not the wind would drop and allow us to "get a few more miles in". Perhaps a more disciplined approach was needed. But at the time there were so many other things to consider: like the miles left to do, and the days left to paddle and so on. Nothing about this expedition was easy. In fact, there were numerous headaches - from its sponsorships and its organisation to its paddling.

SIX WEEKS AFTER

14th October 1994

I was leading a group of schoolboys on a three-day mountaineering trip. We camped on the Pembroke coast.

It was noticeable how I'd almost forgotten how to erect the Dragon, taking 20 minutes or so fumbling in the fading light. Once inside, it seemed odd to be on my own, with no Leon to talk to. The sounds outside were those of the sea and the wind which I'd become so used to hearing, and I began to drift back to the expedition remembering all the fun and freedom it had offered.

On my return, the Head Master at Eton had said: "As time drifts by, you'll start to forget the heartache and pain of such a journey and choose to remember the romance and magic such an expedition evokes." This was already happening.

AROUND FOUR MONTHS LATER

22nd March 1995

Rarely a day goes by when I do not think about my expedition and float back into its simple, calm world or indeed someone asks me about it.

I now look back and can better digest those 67 days and nights of my life that revolved exclusively around the sea and her moods and, of course, the effect on my moods. The extremes of such fear I have never felt or experienced before, and in doing so I had to cope with this fear. I think that as intelligent animals our greatest, or worst, fear is that of losing our life. This, as I have mentioned where appropriate in this book, is a fear I met head-on and had to come to terms with or I would have surely perished. I am sure many of you reading this have in other ways felt that feeling and also addressed it. I am not unique in that, but I do not wish to belittle it.

There were extremes of complete ecstasy in achieving a set goal, often against unbelievable odds. But for every high moment, one knew a low one would follow.

I often relied on Leon, and he on me, when these moments came and moods decreased or removed drive and motivation. When fear clouded judgement, when exhaustion or fatigue made one's will to continue dwindle, when the weather prevented any progress, damaging already tender confidence. When lack of hygiene, dirty clothes or paddling in a urine-soiled canoe or personal grooming caused lowering of self-esteem. When boredom caused anxiety, when hunger caused irrationality, when pain caused frustration and aggression. On all of these occasions, we bolstered each other acting as a mental crutch for one another.

A symbiotic relationship grew. A relationship so in balance that one thought, felt, and decided for the other in a selfless and undemanding manner. This very special bond, created of necessity, was something I have never felt before or since. We are indebted to each other, for in 67 days together we were as one and not two separate entities. We were a most unique team.

I always suspected, but now know for certain, the mind is far stronger than that of its counterpart, the physical body. I do not mean this was not an incredibly physical challenge, because it most definitely was. However without man's mind, the physical body is useless. It is like a car without its driver: motionless and redundant. It was our minds that pulled us through this gruelling physical experience. One's mental approach affects motivation and drive. These are the two single most powerful forces we all possess. If you have a positive mental approach almost anything is possible. One's horizon is indeed without limit.

By putting myself through such an ordeal, I find, I have a much more positive approach to life. I've learnt better how to adapt to any given situation, to work as part of a team. To be confident in one's approach, to be able to motivate yourself and others, even under pressure. To be more rational. To not limit one's experiences and above all be humble, learning from other people's experiences.

On a final note. One should never limit one's horizons or worse, let someone else limit them. We are what we achieve, not what others perceive. Only our perception of achievement is important.

APPENDIX I

BIG HUGS AND THANKS

This whole 67-day expedition was financed on a shoestring budget. Without the help of our sponsors it would not have been possible. Even when we had all our equipment stolen, our sponsors were on standby to once again pitch in. I sincerely thank them for their generosity and invaluable support.

Admiralty Charts – Ainsworth – Aquascribe – Mr Arbitor, Arbitor Group plc – Calagne – Clarke & Co, Eton – Coleman UK – Coleman Taymar Ltd – Dunfold – Fender – First Ascent – Gul International – Holland & Aitchison – Imray Lauria Norie & Wilson Ltd – W.A.Ingram Association Ltd – Jack Wolfskin – Konica – Lam-Fold – Maxless – Merrell – Murphy's Irish Stout – Nookie Kayaking equipment – Olympus UK – Pains-Wessex – Photo Optix – Stella Sealink - Thermarest - Vaurnet – Zeiss – Zippo.

En route, we were treated on numerous occasions to hospitality fit for gods - ranging from cream buns in Gweedor Post Office to a night in a four-poster bed in Glin Castle. To all those who took pity and helped us – THANK YOU.

Granny McNamee – Ann & Oliver Stowey – Ivan Sutton, Kilmore Quay – the Nolan family, Co Dublin – Charles Blanford, Howth Yacht Club – the Breatnach family, Co.Waterford – Frank & Mandy Losruohan, Co.Dublin – Bobby Clancy of The Clancy Brothers – Bill Clancy, Co Waterford – Donovan – James, Carolyn, Crispin, Magnus and Faith Dyer – The Garvin family – Paddy & Mark Magner, Co Clear – The Knights of Glyn & Dedra – Stephen Hannon and all at Little Killary Adventure Centre – The Irish Tourist Board – Bill & Elizabeth Masser – Mrs Rigby – The Ralston family – Mary McFadden, Meenlargh Post Office – Robert, Lorelly & Phoo Forrester – Kate & Owen.

Others for their help and support in numerous ways:

Chris Jones – Mike Town – Brian Graham, Adare Productions – Kevin Ross & Suzanne Weston, Eton School of Mechanics – Nigel Dennis, A.S.S.C Wales – Alan Price – Dr Eric Anderson – John Vessey – George Fussey – Nick Hitchcock – Johnny Noakes – Carol Cocker – Guy Birt – Angus Graham-Campbell – Wallis Clark – Mike Weigt – Tom Wheelon – David Guilford – Simon Vivian – Russell Polden – Paddy Gilson and Nick Devereux for contributing their artwork to this book – Alan Ward, Philip McCosker – British Canoe Union – Andy Middleton – Alan Price – June Wells for typing this book from a pile of garb into something legible – The Eton College PE Department, Glen Pierce, Andy Halladay and Phil Macleod, for putting up with an overexcited 'canoe bore' and a very special thanks to my mother and father. I know Mum had numerous sleepless nights and tense moments throughout this 67-day expedition; I also know my father had the job of keeping her calm. Both in their own way helped me to complete the journey.

Bill Masser, from the very mention of this expedition, was full of good ideas, a wealth of knowledge and experience on the canoeing front and the coastal waters of Ireland. But, greater than all this, was his immense enthusiasm and passion for us to succeed in our adventure. Thanks Bill.

Lastly, to our loyal and cherished friend Cathy 'Gigi' Gilson. Her part in our expedition became almost as great as ours. She flew out to see us three times, lifting our tender spirits, willing us to achieve our final goal. For all this, I whole-heartedly offer my sincere thanks.

APPENDIX II

KIT WE USED

Kayak

We both chose, after much deliberation I might add, Nigel Dennis's design of sea kayak called 'The Romany', named, he told me, after his daughter. It appealed to us both, for a number of reasons:

Its revolutionary large key-hole cockpit made landings easier with extra space in the deck, allowing slick evacuation from the boat. I've always found the usual, small hole, a nightmare. Access onto the water was also much easier.

The 3-hatch design slit the boat into three areas. This is always a bonus: wet, smelly kit or fuel can be kept away from dry kit or food. The number of times you hear of fuel leaking and spoiling a week's food rations - this certainly prevents this. I had camping kit at back, food and maps in middle and dry clothes in front. Leon had the same, except for the middle which housed fuel and cooking equipment. The main hatch openings are easily large enough to stow bigger items, such as a tent or stove.

Stability, durability and speed – laden or unladen, the Romany was very stable and easy to manoeuvre even in rough water and we hit some shit-rough water. The Romany was battered by numerous rough rocky launches or landings in surf and the like. The boats were often dropped in portage by weary paddlers. Generally, they cruised at four knots on average.

Comfortable spongy seat, if you are at sea for extended periods at a time, a comfy seat is a must. These seats moulded to your bottom, keeping it very comfortable and warm – no piles I'm pleased to add!

Adjustable foot rests, the type found in a play boat, which allowed fine-tuning depending on the sea state and weather. It also allowed the odd leg stretch en route which believe me, is important on long days.

The hatches were easy to get on and off (we cleaned and lubricated the seals every three to four days with Johnson's baby Vaseline - great smell!) even with cold numb hands, and never once leaked. We were so confident in their watertight ability after the second week, dry bags were never closed, becoming almost obsolete. A boat I would unreservedly recommend and indeed use again. A long-awaited revolutionary design in sea kayaks.

Repairs
Only one major repair needing fibreglass, due to vandalism on our boats. Leon had a slight leak, but tape and Vaseline applied every week or so cured most of it.

Paddles
I used a Lendal Power Master – it was light, durable and strong. I certainly gave it a hard time. It stood up very well.
Leon used Ainsworth K106 Spec 2 – racing paddle. It seemed to stand up to the journey better, but was a little heavier. Both extremely good paddles.

Buoyancy Aids
I used a Foster Rowe Sea Instructor's buoyancy aid as it was designed especially for the sea canoeist. I was bitterly disappointed in its performance. I found it cumbersome and pedantic, with its over-emphasis on complicated pockets and buckles, making it difficult to find emergency quick release. Its colours also faded quickly.

The idea of a fanny bag to carry distress flares sounds good in principle, but in practice the distress flares didn't fit very well. The added top-heavy weight made rolling and general balance difficult. It's a rather flashy buoyancy aid with numerous buckles and zips that didn't really marry up. Simple is probably best. A definite mistake.

Leon used Perry's Pullover vest. It concentrated on doing the job of a comfortable buoyancy aid and did it well – a good choice.

Spray decks
Nookie Neoprene keyhole deck – tough, hard-wearing and watertight – very impressed.

Canoe Clothing
We both used **Nookie** – long-sleeved semi-dry cags. Excellent kit, warm, dry and hard-wearing – saved our skin on barnacle beach landings many times – I'd recommend them, also nice colours.
I also packed a short-sleeved **Gortex Palm semi-dry cag**. I wore it almost non-stop. I liked the extra freedom it gave to the arms whilst keeping the main part of the torso dry and warm. I also had a great suntan on my arms!

We both wore **Duofold** long-sleeved thermal tops and were very impressed; they kept us continually warm, even when wet and sodden. The tops were also quick drying. We both agreed Duofold long-sleeved tops were our favourite, most versatile piece of kit. Worn on all 67 days of the expedition, at sea, on land and whilst asleep. I cannot recommend them highly or strongly enough. In fact, I recently found out Randolf Fiennes wore one on his unassisted crossing of the Antarctic.

Jack Wolfskin Fleece Hats – excellent wearing; warm when wet plus quick drying.

Varlite Sun Glasses – these were hard-wearing shades, keeping our eyes protected from U.V. light. They were dropped on rocks, in the sea, sat on and still kept going – they also look good!

GULL Shortie Wet Suit – 67 days of wear and tear through thick and thin. An excellent and recommended piece of kit – invaluable. Keeping us warm and protected.

Footwear – Leon – Gull Booties / Cathal – Merrell Sandals: both perform very well

DRY LAND CLOTHING

Jack Wolfskin supplied the expedition with fleece tops and bottoms – Gortex breathable waterproofs, aptly named 'cats and dogs'. These were high performance bits of kit, essential with the notorious ever-changing Irish climate. The fleece tops were worn on all 67 days of the expedition. We were kept warm and dry thanks to this high standard gear.

Duofold – Windproof Fleece Jackets – again an essential, durable, warm, versatile and exceptionally well-designed piece of kit. It was worn non-stop on land – its numerous pockets housed everything we owned.

Sealine Waterproof Dry Bags – we used a number of different shapes and sizes to keep our kit dry. Some were more durable and hard-wearing than others but generally very good quality bags – I did prefer the see-through ones as kit could be more easily found – good cushions for back whilst paddling – we both had a dual purpose ruck-sack design sealed dry bag, which was great for carrying kit on land, an excellent idea, that I'm sure will catch on.

Camping – NB – we never once used a torch, just fumbled in the dark, not finding it a problem.

Colman Stove – fast, efficient and took a beating. I'm used to using a Trangia, so the stove was a real eye opener; it was fast, efficient and the heat was easy to control, so no burnt scrambled eggs! Needless to say, it was kicked around and stood up well. The Colman Cooking kit was small, light and did the job.

Jack Wolfskin Tent – Dragon – Amazing, it took us an average three minutes to erect. It was incredibly durable, standing up to gale force winds, sea water, attacks by cows, being roughly packed and unpacked; it was even used as a Wendy Play House by small children en route. Its internal design made it warm and well ventilated, enabling wet/damp kit to be hung up to dry. I would wholeheartedly recommend it.

I have used many types, shapes and different makes of tent on numerous university and school mountaineering/camping trips. But I have not found a tent as easy, tough and reliable as this one.

Bedding – Thermarest – sleep is so important on this type of expedition. A good night's kip can be the difference between being capable of enjoying a day's paddle or not and hating it. We both found our Thermarest comfier than a bed. It was also light, easily packable and durable. I will never camp again without it.

Repair Kit – we tried to cater for most situations. Luckily, we did not need to put much of this equipment to the test. In the event of a repair to the kayaks, we carried the following items in waterproof containers:

> 2lb laminating resin; quantity of catalyst; 2 square yards of chopped strand mat and webbed; 2 x 2 inch brushes; 1 roll of black carpet tape (3 inch); spare cord/plumber's tape; plastic gloves (four pairs); a dry cloth; methylated spirit; Zippo lighter; sharp knife; sharpener.

Spare Kit – (i)   4 boat hatches (2 small and 2 large).
　　　　　　(ii)   4 spray decks (2 Neoprene and 2 plastic).
　　　　　　(iii) 4 woolly hats (I hate a cold head).
　　　　　　(iv)   2 sets of split paddles.

APPENDIX III

GRUB WE ATE

It is true that canoeing offers little chance for the large leg muscles to be totally active, but the long days – with much of the activity outside of the boat and in the upper body – merit high calorie intake. Also of concern was the need to keep our bodies 'built up' in the later stages, but more importantly, 'building up' in the early stages. So a balanced diet is required of about 5,000 to 6,000 calories per day.

After reading and asking other people who had been on similar expeditions, we decided to buy our food en route. Lunch would usually be made by us, but evening meals wherever possible would be bought in pubs and restaurants. We felt this decision was solid for three reasons: food takes time and patience to cook, which we felt would be better spent exploring and enjoying Ireland and its culture; the food is almost as cheap to buy prepared as to buy in its uncooked state; and we wanted to relax and enjoy at least one meal a day, not having to rush it in the rain or eat in our smelly tent.

Main meals, lunch and supper (neither of us ate breakfast regularly) consisted of carbohydrates – complex and simple – fats and protein. Namely chicken and chips followed by treacle tart, or Irish stew and spuds followed by apple pie and cream. Snacks on the water inevitably were high in calorific value and small in size – usually chocolate, biscuits, cake and bananas. This we hoped would give the high calorific balanced diet we needed. Fluid on the sea was fresh water or as fresh as we could get. On land, usually tea, coffee and the odd Murphy's.

The choice of food in the shops that we encountered was excellent and it would be true to say that we had a varied and interesting diet. However, we both lost a considerable amount of weight: I personally lost over a stone and I do not really have a lot of surplus weight normally. I suppose that a certain degree of weight loss is inevitable, taking into account the high calorific output involved in expedition sea canoeing, but over a stone seems excessive. It therefore seems obvious even with this diet that we were not eating enough of the right kinds of food with high calorific values.

We both found ourselves having to force food down, leading to an unpleasant full to bursting feeling, in an attempt to try and prevent any further weight loss. It is true to say, eating for the first time ever became a chore.

I stated earlier, neither of us ate breakfast regularly. This was due to two reasons: we do not like eating just after waking; and more importantly, if we missed breakfast we could be on the water paddling within half an hour. This we felt gave us a mental edge on the day. I hated fussing about; I just wanted to put in some miles straight away.

We both took fishing lines with us. We found them cumbersome as our speed of transit would not allow for this kind of relaxed pleasure; occasionally we did trawl for mackerel. The only thing we seemed to catch were other fishermen's nets, so we abandoned this quaint notion quite early on in the expedition.

One other point to note, our teeth took a beating. The amount of rich and sugary food we ate must have taken its toll, even brushing two or three times a day.

APPENDIX IV

DEAR DOCTOR ...

Safety Kit between us – we carried one personal distress beacon, 4 parachute distress flares – 4 red smoke distress flares – 4 white smoke distress flares (unfortunately, some stolen and flares let off in Easkey, Co. Sligo). A personal distress beacon sends out a continual distress signal and location, when activated, to a satellite which sends it to the appropriate coastguard, who addresses a rescue. I informed the coastguard in Dublin of our expedition, its route and the safety kit we were carrying. We did not phone in to the coastguard on a daily basis, as we decided it would be too much hassle and removed the puritanical approach to sea kayaking and our expedition.

First Aid (stolen in Easkey, Co. Sligo)
The amount of medical equipment taken was minimal. If there was a major problem, local hospitals or doctors were relatively close at hand, as I found out. Our kit contained the following:

> Emergency telephone numbers of all coast and rescue teams in Ireland; next of kin; money (coins) for telephone; assorted melolin absorbent dressings; 1 triangular bandage; a crepe bandage; assorted safety pins; 2 x 2 inch conforming bandage; 1 packet absorbent lint; 1 pack skin closures; 1 box Strepsils; 2 rolls adhesive tape; assorted Dennis the Menace plasters; scissors; lipsalve; assorted painkillers; and sunburn cream.

We were fortunate enough to need very few of these items: headache tables, sunburn cream and lipsalve only. The main problems were headaches (through dehydration and sunlight) and general aches and pains, although these decreased as the trip progressed and we became fitter. I would on future expeditions recommend jellyfish/insect bite cream and diarrhoea medication, as both were needed on this expedition.

APPENDIX V

BODIES ON THE LINE

Incidence of ill health

Being in the sea for long periods caused the skin on our hands to absorb water, so that they were completely waterlogged; the human skin can absorb five times its own weight of water. This caused our hands to be continuously wet or damp on land, making the skin very soft and thus susceptible to cuts and nicks by abrasion with the boats, rocks etc. We both noticed packing and unpacking the boats caused most of our hands' cuts and nicks. It was also noticeable that our tactile senses were lessened, finding it difficult to feel small objects. I would liken this feeling to having numb fingers and hands. Together with this, there was a reduction in skin sensitivity, also caused by the quantity of water absorbed; this meant we did not notice the damage to our skin for some time. The continuous drenching that any wounds received caused the healing process to be slowed and this exacerbated the problem.

Both of us suffered a frequency of muscle pain in our arms, shoulders and general upper body. We especially found, after a long day's paddle, our stomach or abdominal muscles could not support the upper torso when seated. Thus we needed chairs which had support for backs at times, even this was not enough; we found the only solution was to lay flat on the floor.

Blisters

The evidence of blisters was very low considering the length of time we actually spent holding the paddles. This can only be attributed to the fact that our paddles were of the highest quality.

Diarrhoea

We both suffered diarrhoea from time to time, draining fluids and energy from our already weary bodies. I suffered diarrhoea and vomiting for three to four days towards the end. It almost finished the trip for me.

Tenosynovitis
On separate occasions, we both suffered from pains in the wrist which immediately caused concern. However, these pains didn't last for extended periods. It can only be concluded that these pains were not due to tenosynovitis.

Breaks (bones) and serious damage
There was no breakage of bones or serious cuts requiring stiches during this expedition.

Backs
Lower back pain was common in the coccyx. It soon became obvious to us both that making sure our back-rest dry bags were in a comfy position and supporting our backs was essential. At night, we found it difficult to sleep on our fronts, which was our usual sleeping posture.

We had to lie down on our back with our legs bent to support our coccyx, eventually letting out legs straighten, then finally rolling onto our side before dozing off. This became a nightly ritual, as it was the only way to regain comfort and get to sleep.

Visits to Doctor
I visited a doctor, Dr Heggety, on one occasion because a parasite was causing opening and bleeding on an old appendix scar. It was probably caused by lack of personal hygiene, limited showering and so on, perhaps inevitable on this type of expedition.

Hernia
On some of the rougher days, Leon's hernia did cause him some problems, manifesting in pain and tightening of this thigh and stomach muscles. We did have to stop early on a few occasions.

APPENDIX VI

NAVIGATION, TIDES AND WEATHER

I initially gained all the nautical charts necessary to cover Ireland's coast. These were kindly given to the expedition by two different publishers; this caused slight problems as the scales differed. I also obtained Ordnance Survey maps of Ireland's coast from the Irish Tourist Board.

Some of the charts were made of a 'revolutionary' wax waterproof paper, so I did not have them laminated. Every other map and chart, I did. We found the laminated ones could put up with any amount of wet wear and tear, but the 'so called' wax waterproof paper could not, instead disintegrating very quickly. En route to Dungarvan , we photocopied the remains of the rather shabby and soggy waxed charts and laminated them. We had no further problems.

Until our charts and maps were stolen in Co. Sligo, one of us carried the charts of the area on our deck, usually me, and the other had the Ordnance Survey map, usually Leon. This meant I kept an eye out for tidal races, islands and so on, while Leon would spot towns and possible lunch stops. It was possible to use only the OS map on the expedition, as it gave sufficient information of topography; we ended up having to do this after Co. Sligo. Both boats had an area designated to carry and stick a compass. We decided Leon should carry his close at hand and mine should be on the boat. I also carried a hand-held compass in my buoyancy aid - this turned out to be a good plan, as in an emergency rescue my compass was lost. We used our compasses regularly, as fog and mist were rather prevalent on the coast. The navigation was relatively basic, although it's worth noting that the numerous islands around Connemara were not all charted; this did lead to slight confusion at times. Wherever possible, we would ask the locals for advice, sometimes we took it and sometimes ignored it, but it was always useful to have it. I would say most fishermen would not apply their knowledge to our craft, but to their own (usually motor trawlers) so we had to make the adjustments.

Tides and Weather

We didn't take the tides into account on the south, west or north as the tidal range is so small.

On the east, however, it is large enough to matter so we found its assistance a definite advantage. We did not have tide tables, instead using our experience to guesstimate high and low tide: it was usually accurate. We did gain predicted weather forecasts most of the way, but generally used our own ability to judge, sometimes to our definite disadvantage, but mostly we got it right. Our tent was a good judge of the wind speed and direction as it had the ability to bend in numerous directions; we soon became experts at interpreting it all, often without having to leave our sleeping bags.

APPENDIX VII

PHOTOGRAPHY

We both wanted to record this expedition by both still and moving pictures, after all a picture paints a thousand words.

STILL PHOTOGRAPHY

The expedition was sponsored by Olympus in the form of two weatherproof cameras (AFI minis) and Konica helped in the form of 50 rolls of 36 exposure 100/200 ASA films. The cameras were both auto-focus, one having a 200mm lens, which hopefully would give close-ups. Although weatherproof, Olympus did express concern that they may not last if exposed to rough seas. This concern manifested itself around four days into the trip when I became fully submerged with the 200mm lens camera around my neck. Alas, no more close-ups and a roll of photographs lost! Leon's camera lasted considerably longer. It was kept in a semi-dry pouch on his boat deck, but after six weeks it too bit the dust, again losing a roll of photographs. It is important that, for the action picture, the camera had to be carried somewhere easily accessible, inevitably this meant it would be wet more often than not.

With both cameras now useless, we had to find another as soon as possible; every day without a camera, we were missing good photographs. It was unfortunate that we could not find a replacement camera for two weeks due to our general remoteness and lack of days off to shop. Eventually, in Donegal, after spotting a tiny shop in an even tinier back street I found a Canon waterproof Prima AS -1 camera for £170. Its performance was superb, not only was it hard-wearing and completely waterproof, it also took very good quality photographs. With hindsight, this was the camera that we should have taken from the outset of the expedition.

I would give the following advice to anyone wishing to record anything of this nature in the form of photographs: make sure both people have a camera on them at all times, on and off the water. We missed numerous shots due to not having a camera with us all the time. Both people need one, as everyone sees different settings and situations in different ways – gaining a range of photos. It is also, often, too much of a hassle to get the camera from the other person, so inevitably you don't bother, or the subject has moved on by the time you do.

It is essential that the job of photographer is equally taken on by each member of the expedition. When one member stops to snap, all must stop and wait. It takes an awful amount of exertion to catch up with the rest of the party and if it happens too often you lose heart, thereafter no longer stopping to take photos. All this did occasionally happen on this expedition.

MOVING PHOTO FOOTAGE

I bought a £1500 Sony High 8 Camera, on the advice of a number of people, including Adare Television Productions, who were hoping to put a documentary film together about the expedition. Sony recommended a waterproof housing, which would take the knocks and would most definitely stay waterproof. It seemed odd that when the camera was in the casing it did not really fit snugly, more of an awkward squash.

Right from day one it gave us problems; needless to say it leaked profusely even with the slightest exposure to water. It continuously misted up, so footage taken was useless. Its external safety switch kept turning the camera off, inevitably just when you wanted to film something exciting. After numerous phone calls to Sony, they assured us it worked and they would test the housing if we sent it to them. They also told us it would take around six weeks. I did explain we were in the middle of an expedition and to lose the camera for one day was bad enough, but to lose it for up to six weeks would be impossible. Sony's after-sales service, I found less than unsatisfactory.

After practically covering the camera and its housing in pots of Vaseline, it did start to work better and if very carefully handled footage could be gained.

I would not recommend this camera or use it again, the

combination of its incompatibility with its housing and Sony's lack of help made it a headache from start to finish. I should add the camera died in the seventh week of the expedition, highlighting its unsuitability for this type of water adventure.

I guess it might be okay in a drought!

Cathy on a windswept visit

Leon - enjoying the sun

A lighthouse in a remote spot

Getting ready for another day - looking at the charts

We have turned into wild men!

An early start.
We always paddled for a couple of hours then had
breakfast, as neither of us woke ready to eat

Another Headland, looking for the overfalls

**Where have our bellies gone?
We both lost weight on the trip**

Front Cover: a choppy day at sea, staying close to each other in case of a rescue

An old wreck on the West Coast

The calmest sunniest day of the adventure

The tide went out

An abandoned house on the coast, perfect for lunch

Another soft day in Ireland

Back at Eton's outdoor pool with ' The Daily Telegraph'

Testing the new boats and sponsorship equipment

Lots of birds on the West Coast

Meeting Donovan, old Mellow Yellow himself and jamming a few tunes

Little Phoo Forester trying out our lifejacket

**Personal hygiene -
Cathal brushing his teeth after a day at sea**

**A typical start to the day:
packed up - even our guitars on the boats**

APPENDIX VIII

EXPEDITION TRIVIA

In 67 days, we each:
- Consumed 250 bars of chocolate (the calories consumed from the chocolate were 62,500 for each of us);
- Spent £75 on chocolate;
- Drank 167 litres of water;
- Drank 140 litres of tea; around 300 pots of tea;
- Drank 10 litres of coffee; around 50 mugs of coffee;
- Drank 70 pints of Murphy's stout (4 bottles of Murphy's Red!);
- Ate 82 slices of apple pie with cream or ice cream (approximately 28,000 calories for each of us);
- Ate 30 pounds of cheese;
- Ate 10 loaves of bread;
- Ate 6 pounds of butter;
- Ate 35 tins of rice pudding;
- Ate 15 tins of baked beans (causing extreme flatulence);
- Ate 60 packets of biscuits;
- Ate 130 bananas; and
- Ate 5 apples.
- The average number of calories per day to keep us kayaking was 4,500 to 5,000 each – a total of 301,000 to 335,000 each.

Paddling
- Total distance covered – 1,200 miles.
- Number of paddle strokes – 3,600 / hour.
- Number of paddle strokes – 21,600 / day.
- Average time in the boats – 6 hours / day
- Total time in the boats – 390 hours.
- Shortest time in the boats – 25 minutes.
- Longest time in the boats – 9.5 hours.
- Number of capsizes – 1 by Cathal.
- Number of emergency rescues – 1 for Cathal.
- Number of repairs made – 3.
- Number of rough/difficult landings – too many: 26!

- Average mileage per day – 17.9 – therefore x 67 = 1,200 in total.
- Number of rest days – 10.
- Number of storm days – 7.
- Number of days actually paddling – 50.

Hospitality
- Free pints – 16 each.
- Free meals – 37 each.
- Free beds – 21 each.
- Nights spent in tent – 38.
- Nights spent in paid accommodation – 8.
- Best hospitality received - along the south coast.
- Hitched lifts – 70.
- Average walk to pub from campsite – 2 miles.
- Longest walk to pub – 16 miles.
- Shortest walk to pub – 160 yards.
- Average hours sleep per night – 10.
- Total sleep whole trip – 670 hours.

Wild Life Encountered
- Number of seals spotted – 400 or more.
- Number of dolphins (including Fungi in Dingle Bay) – 5
- Number of basking sharks – only 1 thank God!
- Number of seagulls – 1,000s.
- Number of cormorants – 100s.
- Number of guillemots – 100s.
- Number of shags – 100s.
- Number of cows – 1,000s.
- Number of sheep and lambs - 1,000s

Personal Hygiene
- Number of times clothes washed – 3 times.
- Teeth brushed – once per day on average.
- Showers – every ten days on average.
- Longest without a shower – 2.5 weeks – we stank!
- Hair-wash with shampoo – not once in 67 days.
- Haircut – we preferred to look like wild men.

- Average number of earwigs/creepy crawlies found on us or in our clothing – 2 per day each.
- Number of shaves – 5 Cathal and 7 Leon.
- Most irritating and repetitive problem – sore bottoms.

Clothing
- No of hats/caps lost – Cathal 6 and Leon 2.
- Favourite piece of kit – Duofold Thermal top, worn on all 67 days of expedition.
- No of pairs of underwear used – Cathal 1 and Leon 2.

Miscellaneous
- Weight loss – Cathal 1 stone 8lbs; and Leon gained half a stone!
- Number of pay phones used – 82.
- Number of postcards sent – Cathal 31 and Leon 20.
- Number visits to toilet – 70 each.
- Number visits to open-air toilet – 150 each.
- Number of Irish counties passed through – 16 out of a possible 32.
- Average number of sunny days – 38.
- Average number of wet days – 49.
- Average number of windy days – 22.
- Number of times rained on while changing into dry kit – 54 days out of 67 days.
- Average time to erect tent – 3 minutes.
- Number of times cooked on a stove – 5.

Worst moment
- Cathal – launching and finding I'd been covered in jellyfish stings.
- Leon – paddling for our lives in Ratlin Sound.

Questions most frequently asked by enquiring natives (all about 6,000 times each!)
- How far do you paddle each day?
- How do you go for a pee when in your canoe?
- How close do you canoe to shore?
- Do you sleep in your boat?

- Where do you keep your food and equipment?
- How many times have you capsized?
- Are you mad?
- Would you like a cup of tea?
- Why are you doing this?
- Is it a two-man canoe?

Things missed most
- Freedom to relax in your own space (environment).
- Cups of tea at will.
- Showers.
- Car.
- Rest.

Things missed least
- The rat race.
- Trivialities of life.
- My diary.

APPENDIX IX

THE BEAUFORT WIND SCALE

Force	Knots	Called	Sea Conditions	Sea state	Canoeists
0	1 or less	Calm	Like a mirror	Smooth	
1	1-3	Light air	Ripples like scales	Calm	Suitable for beginners under instruction
2	4-6	Light breeze	Small wavelets, glassy crests, not breaking	Calm	Suitable for beginners under instruction
3	7-10	Gentle breeze	Large wavelets, crests begin to break, glassy foam	Calm	Proficiency standard
4	11-16	Moderate breeze	Small waves, becoming longer, fairly frequent white horses	Slight	Paddlers should be OK
5	17-21	Fresh breeze	Moderate waves, more pronounced long form, many white horses, possibly some spray	Moderate	Over proficiency standard
6	22-27	Strong breeze	Large waves begin to form, white crests more extensive everywhere, probably some spray	Rather rough	Advanced paddlers only
7	28-33	Near gale	Sea heaps up with white foam from breaking waves	Rather rough	Advanced paddlers probably wishing they had got a forecast…
8	34-40	Gale	Moderately high waves of greater length, much foam	Rough	
9	41-47	Strong gale	High waves, dense streaks of foam along the direction of wind	Very rough	
10	48-55	Storm			
11	56-65	Severe storm			
12	66+	Hurricane			

APPENDIX X

PRESS CUTTINGS AND GUINNESS BOOK OF RECORDS CERTIFICATE

THE DAILY TELEGRAPH

AN ETON master will spend the summer kayaking around Ireland. In the manner of a Victorian off on the Grand Tour, Cathal McCosker will not be travelling light. Into his kayak will go tweeds, golf clubs and a guitar.

McCosker, 26, a gym teacher, will be accompanied by a sporty friend, Leon Harris. They came up with the idea of circumnavigating Ireland "over a few Guinesses" last year. It was the beauty of the Irish coast that grabbed them, its wildlife, and the thought of soda bread, so good after a salty day on summer seas.

Along the way they hope to drop in on the Duke of Devonshire at Lismore Castle in Co Waterford (hence the tweeds) and the Sixties singer Donovan in Co Cork (hence the guitar). There may also be some golf, and other Irish traditions. A practice trip to the Aran islands, for instance, was delayed when they were invited into a pub at three in the afternoon. They emerged 12 hours later, eyes like paddles.

Well paddled: Harris and McCosker

20 MONDAY, SEPTEMBER 12, 1994

THE DAILY TELEGRAPH

Up the creek

TWO canoeists who in June set out to circumnavigate Ireland have just completed their journey. On the trip Cathal McCosker and Leon Harris were stung by jellyfish, charged by a bull, suffered sunstroke — and nearly shot to ribbons.

One day they were paddling up an estuary (name withheld) when they noticed green Land Rovers racing about on the beach, flashing their lights. McCosker recalls: "I paddled up to investigate and this man shouted: 'Do you realise where you are? We've got a bloody shooting range here. Do you want to get shot?' I told him it wasn't on the chart and he yelled back: 'That's because it's a secret.'"

ROUND IRELAND BY KAYAK

NAVIGATORS CONQUER THE EMERALD ISLE

36

Eton College instructors Cathal McCosker and Leon Harris have earned a place in *The Guinness Book Of Records* for circumnavigating Ireland in two kayaks. It was a pipe dream that became a reality for the young adventurers after 67 days of blood, sweat and a few scrapes that had them dicing with death.

But as you'd expect of any trip to the hospitable Emerald Isle, there were also the good times, during their periodic breaks on dry land to recharge their batteries.

The two were lucky enough to stumble upon the last Knight of Glyn's romantic, ancestral castle in County Limerick .

"We were probably the smelliest wild men he had ever entertained," Cathal grins mischievously. And he may well have a point, since by the time they made it to his castle they had forsaken any semblance of appearing civilised. While racing their kayaks to meet their record-breaking goal, grooming had gone out of the window.

In Cork, they ran into the Sixties folk idol Donovan with whom they enjoyed a jamming session and in Waterford they shared a pint or two with Bobby Clancy of the Clancy Brothers and Tommy Makim.

But the two sportsmen had some hairy encounters. On the Dingle Peninsula, notorious for its 40-foot Atlantic sea swells, they realised that death was a real possibility. "The sheer size of this wall of water from our tiny craft was my most vivid experience during the whole trip. We were like two corks bobbing in a violent jacuzzi," Cathal recalls. "I accepted the reality of being so close to death and this kept me going."

Pipe dream into reality: Leon Harris and Cathal McCosker with their kayaks

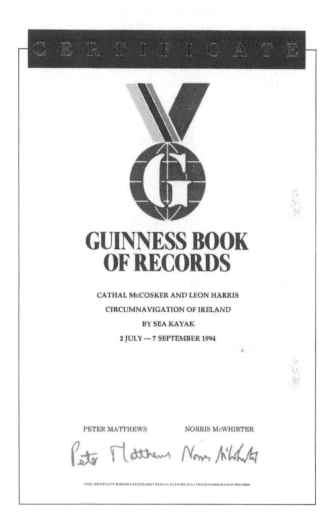

AUTHOR BIOGRAPHY

At university, Cathal McCosker was taken on a rather exciting paddle out to sea, returning by R.N.L.I. helicopter.

He's taught at Eton, Cothill and in Cape Town. He's led many expeditions with his pupils, and nearly froze on Snowdon in winter when he forgot his sleeping bag! He believes life is an adventure – in a kayak or sitting at a desk or in the pub, anything can happen. He's also paddled around Corsica, Scotland and Pembrokeshire.

He lives in the country with his wife, children and three dogs.

10551809R00117

Printed in Great Britain
by Amazon.co.uk, Ltd.,
Marston Gate.